TEACHING UNITS FOR TURNED-OFF TEENS

Classroom Activities for Secondary School Students

by EUGENIA SACOPULOS and MARJORIE GIBSON

is a book that helps you bridge the gap between the interests and concerns of teenagers and the traditional secondary school curriculum. Complete, classroom-tested activities sustain students' attention because they are built around areas such as understanding oneself and getting along with others, solving problems and making choices, career direction, music, cars, astrology, ecology, maturity and modern mores.

Each learning experience helps young people improve their self-image, enhance their communications skills, and relate academic accomplishments to their everyday lives and to their future careers.

ALL PRE-PLANNED AND READY TO USE!

These teaching units include everything you need for exciting classroom lessons:

Preliminary strategies that set the stage for the unit

Directions for establishing a dialogue

Guidelines for discussion

Examples, illustrations, sample forms, and suggested readings

No large budgets, no elaborate equipment, no extensive preparations are needed! These activities have all been pre-planned and tested for you in the classroom by skilled and experienced teachers.

ACTIVITIES FOR EVERY ABILITY LEVEL

TEACHING UNITS FOR TURNED-OFF TEENS gives you scores of formal and informal activities focusing primarily on English and social studies, but also incorporating the fine arts, mathematics, and science. These units are flexible and adaptable to *any* ability level within Grades 7 to 12 and are especially valuable for youngsters with reading problems.

ACTIVITIES TEACH THE WHOLE STUDENT

TEACHING UNITS FOR TURNED-OFF TEENS builds self-confidence as well as skills that are transferable to other subjects and to life experiences.

Exploration and analysis, critical thinking and responsibility for one's own behavior are stressed in activities that encourage success—that break into the pattern of failure experienced by so many poorly-motivated youngsters.

With this excellent teaching aid, you can reinforce standard curricula and communications skills and demonstrate their importance in the "real world." You can *turn teens on to learning*.

ABOUT THE AUTHORS

EUGENIA SACOPULOS and MARJORIE GIBSON have had extensive experience in all of the grades from junior high to college: Ms. Sacopulos as a guidance counselor and teacher of English and reading; Ms. Gibson as a librarian and media specialist.

Ms. Gibson currently teaches at Purdue University. Ms. Sacopulos is principal of Froebel Junior High School in Gary, Indiana, where both women live.

TEACHING UNITS FOR TURNED-OFF TEENS:

Classroom Activities for Secondary School Students

TEACHING UNITS FOR TURNED-OFF TEENS:

Classroom Activities for Secondary School Students

Eugenia Sacopulos

and

Marjorie Gibson

The Center for Applied Research in Education, Inc.

West Nyack, New York 10994

© 1976, by

THE CENTER FOR APPLIED RESEARCH IN EDUCATION, INC.

West Nyack, New York

Library of Congress Cataloging in Publication Data

Sacopulos, Eugenia,
    Teaching units for turned-off teens.

    Includes bibliographies and index.
    1. Education, Secondary—Curricula—Handbooks,
manuals, etc. 2. Interaction analysis in education.
I. Gibson, Marjorie,   joint author.
II. Center for Applied Research in Education.
III. Title.
LB1607.S32   373.1'3   75-44313
ISBN 0-87628-812-3

Printed in the United States of America

92424

This book is dedicated with much love and affection to
CHARLOTTE and LYNN
and to
BECKY'S MOTHER

ABOUT THE AUTHORS

Eugenia Sacopulos and Marjorie Gibson met when Ms. Sacopulos was a guidance counselor and Ms. Gibson a curriculum librarian at the Tolleston School in Gary, Indiana. They have teamed up here as they did then to share their successful teaching strategies and to explore new ways to motivate teens to learn new skills and improve weak ones.

Both of the writers have had extensive experience at various educational levels. Eugenia Sacopulos has taught English and reading in grades nine through twelve and in adult high school classes. She has directed innovative summer educational programs for junior high school students. Ms. Sacopulos served as a school counselor for seven years before accepting a position in September, 1974 as an administrative assistant at Lew Wallace High School in Gary, Indiana. In July, 1975 she began a new position as principal of Froebel Junior High School. Ms. Sacopulos has published articles in several educational journals.

Besides her work as school librarian at Tolleston School, Marjorie Gibson has been a college librarian and a public librarian. She has also taught library science at Miles College in Birmingham, Alabama and has served as an Associate Professor of Library Science at the Atlanta University Summer School. Ms. Gibson has taught adult high school English classes and has served as an English assistant with Purdue University's Careers Opportunity Program. Mother of two teen-aged daughters, Ms. Gibson works with teens in a multimedia experimental summer program.

About the Practical Values of This Book

The purpose of this book is to help teachers motivate teen-agers to educational achievement by bridging the gap between their interests and the traditional secondary school curriculum. While traditional teaching methods often fail to awaken students' interests, we believe the tools and strategies offered in these units can recycle teens' interests and channel them into academic ac-complishment.

Teaching Units for Turned-off Teens provides complete, ready-to-use, classroom-tested methods and materials that will sustain the attention of secondary school students because they are built around facets of teens' everyday concerns and activities. Under-standing oneself and getting along with others; solving problems and making choices; finding career direction; learning about sex-ual maturity, mores, fantasies, music, cars, astrology, ecology—each subject is used to help young people strengthen their com-munication skills, improve their self-image, and relate educational experiences to their own lives and needs.

The teaching units in this book feature everything the in-novative teacher or administrator needs to implement these lesson plans. Preliminary strategies set the stage for each unit. Directions for establishing a dialogue help even the inexperienced teacher feel comfortable with the activities. And no extensive preparation or large budgets are needed. In fact, all that you may need to proceed with these units is administrative approval of some areas of sen-sitive subject matter.

The strategies presented here do not purport to be a panacea for motivational problems. Rather, they are tools that can help you meet students *where they are*; they can help you show students that you accept them for what they are; that you have confidence in their ability to become what they choose to be.

Teaching Units for Turned-off Teens reinforces standard curricula and basic skills while adding excitement and stimulation to classroom activities. Equally important, however, it provides you with techniques for helping students learn that life is good and that what they learn in school can help them make it better.

Eugenia Sacopulos

Marjorie Gibson

Table of Contents

8. Arousing Students' Interest in the Environment (Continued)

Issues: Dramatic Action • Projects, Challenges, Strategies and Activities • What If . . . • Petitioning for Change • Plan a Complete Class Project • Galvanizing Energy into a Super Project

1

The Rap Renaissance: Teachers, Administrators and Parents Get It Together

The rap renaissance—a whole new era—is in full bloom on the American scene. Rapping, as used in this book, is a way of making keenly felt statements and sharing ideas for improving our day-to-day living. The practice of rapping has become popular in various forms. Late television talk shows often keep our attention even though we struggle to stay awake. Question and answer sections in newspapers have a wide reading public. Small therapy-oriented groups in organizations such as Alcoholics Anonymous, churches, prisons, schools are also successful in helping people find answers and gain the reinforcement they need to handle personal problems with confidence. Educators, too, can use rap sessions to help students to become healthy and productive citizens.

Statistics will doubtless prove that the most successful schools, schools where children are learning and getting along, are not necessarily the most innovative ones, but they are certainly the ones in which an enthusiastic and cooperative spirit exists among all parties concerned—administrators, teachers, parents and students! That's why opening the doors to dialogue in a series of planned rap sessions is important for bringing about change.

OPENING THE DOORS TO DIALOGUE

Everyone in a school setting seems responsible for everything in general and no one seems responsible for anything in particular. Teachers and administrators frequently seem guilty collectively in not reaching children. However, each claims innocence individually. What an impossible situation, you say. Maybe. However; instead of placing blame or making excuses, why not offer positive ways to improve our schools?

It is apparent that what is needed is a *plan* for change within an individual secondary school. A good way to start is by planning a series of rap sessions. The administrator can break the ice by first inviting his staff to an informal "Social (Half) Hour."

Friday, September 28
WHAT'S ON YOUR MIND?
COME AND CHAT!
(Brainstorming, sug-
gesting innovative
ideas, complaining—
All are welcome!)
Faculty Lounge
2:00 - 4:00 P.M.
Refreshments

Aside from the usual complaints regarding paperwork, clerical help, dress codes, student behavior, it is possible that an embryonic philosophy for improving a school may emerge. However, merely setting up a program does not take care of common concerns in education. The barometer of a program's success is the significance it holds as a motivating factor to bring about improvements in the school and in the teaching processes.

Improved communication is the first step.

Several plans can be devised to permit parents and students to voice their suggestions or to air their problems. This may be done either during the day, after school, or in an evening program.

Administrators and teachers may elect to plan a rap session for students during the day. A system can be devised for meeting with specified grades during lunch hours in a nook of the school's materials center or in an empty classroom located near the cafeteria. Pave the way by first rapping with the student council and allowing it to cosponsor the sessions. The student council could invite parents and members of the community to join in these discussions with teachers and administrators. A memo such as the following will set the tone for an informal session:

The 3 R's Are Coming

RAPPORT — Discuss student needs, ask questions, offer suggestions, get to know each other.

REVELATION — Reveal your innermost thoughts about morale, curriculum, school procedures, community resources. Don't be timid about asking questions.

RELAXATION — Punch and cookies.

The emphasis should be on suggestions for improving quality education, and not just on criticism. Constructive criticism is, of course, always welcome. However, students should be encouraged to offer an alternative or to advance a workable solution once a problem has been submitted.

In an evening session, perhaps the school P.T.A. can be invited to act as a cosponsor. In this session, the administrators, teachers, parents and students may all strive to establish common goals for a modified curriculum. All may engage in finding answers to questions like these:

Why are so many "problem" teens repeaters in trouble?

Why is school a dull place to many disadvantaged youth?

Why do so many required courses seem so irrelevant to the sophisticated teen of today?

How do adults *listen* to young people?

Let's get involved. The power lies within each of us to be heard. Let's get our minds together in a "rap renaissance" and come up with ways to make schools happy places to be and places where people learn.

HUMANIZING CLASSROOMS THROUGH IN-SERVICE WORKSHOPS

An in-service workshop to humanize a school and to help ease classroom stress can provide the basis for building an awareness of the impact of teachers' attitudes on their classes and students' attitudes toward their teachers. Counselors and teachers can analyze the types of conduct which interfere with learning, and they can begin to work out ways to modify behavior—their own and their students'.

Teaching is a highly professional role based not only on science but also on art. As teachers work and plan together to exchange ideas and criticism, morale can improve and suggestions for bringing about desired changes in teaching patterns can be generated. A committee of teachers can initiate an in-service training workshop that will help build meaningful communication patterns in a healthy climate.

Here are some guidelines to follow in establishing your workshop.

1. Talk with administrators, counselors, and teachers who indicate a willingness to assist with planning and implementing the workshop.

2. Seek out key faculty members who successfully maintain a healthy classroom atmosphere to serve as catalysts, aides, supporters, and publicists for the program, creating a base for acceptance of the program's goals.

3. Encourage first-year teachers to participate by stressing a team approach. The approach is not "Here is a program you need," but rather, "Let's learn alternative ways to approach problems in the classroom and improve learning activities in our school."

4. Invite specialists on human behavior to serve as moderators of small group discussions (*e.g.* counselors, psychologists, transactional analysis specialists, theologians, and parents.)

5. Recruit teachers who are interested in learning procedures which will help them deal with negative behavior, recognize signs of stress, and reverse stressful situations within classrooms.

6. Focus on ways to improve the learning climate within the classroom. Through systematic observation and recording of stressful situations and a consciousness of workable ones—teachers can learn procedures which will help them deal with negative behavior.

Group participants might meet as follows: The first group, during the lunch hour once a week; the second, after school once a week. The third group might be arranged according to teachers' needs. Sessions should last about twenty-five minutes.

7. Provide a list of suggested readings:

Berne, Eric. *Games People Play.* New York: Grove Press, 1964.
　　　Group Treatment. New York: Grove Press, 1966.
　　　Sex in Human Loving. New York: Simon and Schuster, 1966.
　　　The Structure and Dynamics of Organizations and Groups. New York: Grove Press, 1961.
　　　Transactional Analysis in Psychotherapy. New York: Grove Press, 1971.
　　　What Do You Say After You Say Hello. New York: Grove Press, 1971.

Harris, Thomas A. *I'm Okay: You're Okay.* New York: Harper & Row, 1967.

Jongeward, Dorothy, and Muriel James. *Born to Win.* Reading, Mass.: Addison-Wesley, 1971.

Schiff, Jacqui, and Beth Day. *All My Children.* New York: Pyramid Publications, 1972.

BUILDING A MENTALLY HEALTHY CLASSROOM ATMOSPHERE

Topics for Discussion

1. Attitudes of teachers which inhibit openness in children. Include barriers such as fear of unstructured time; a tendency to make unimportant things seem important; lecturing instead of discussion; nagging, preaching, belittling, humiliating; being judgmental; sounding loud and gruff.

2. Verbal and nonverbal clues which indicate stress *(e.g.,* the signs and symptoms of anger, hostility, and fear).

3. How to share authority and responsibility within the classroom.

4. How to activate pupils' problem-solving and encourage behavior patterns that result in learning without disruptive resistance.

Discussion Openers

What approaches might a teacher use to modify students' behavior patterns when they exhibit attitudes such as these:

Student A..."How far can I go?"

Student A has continued to walk around the room, poke at others around him, even after the teacher has asked him to stop. At one point the teacher thought she heard him call her a jerk. This is a first-year teacher who wants to avoid sending students to the principal's office because she dreads an evaluation that she cannot maintain class discipline. The domino theory sets in, and now it seems as if the entire class is talking and not doing the assignment. It is impossible to carry on with a class discussion. More than half the hour is spent in the teacher's trying to maintain order.

Student B..."What can I do to bug the teacher?"

When the student entered the class early in the semester, the teacher welcomed her questions. She is an above average student. Now she has become a pest. Her favorite saying is, "I'm just not going to do this assignment. It is dumb. I'm not learning anything." Explaining or reasoning with her is useless, since she has become closed minded. She carries arguments to ridiculous ends and makes fun of students who contribute to a discussion. When the teacher avoids calling on Student B, she stops by the desk and asks, "Why are you ignoring me? You show favoritism to other students." Then Student B stops doing any work.

Student C..."See what that dumb teacher made me do!"

Student C enjoys getting out of class to go to the nurse, to the washroom, or to see his counselor. Usually the teacher allows him to leave the classroom in order to have peace in the room when he leaves. When he is in the class, he is always asking the teacher to repeat her remarks, and says he does not understand what is being taught. He slows down the class because he needs so much extra attention. Whenever he fails a test, which is frequently, he blames the teacher for not teaching the material. He compares his answers to his classmates' and suggests that the teacher is prejudiced.

Student D..."Look how hard I've tried."

Every day Student D comes to class on time and looks interested in what is going on. He does no homework outside of class and fails almost every test, but he expects the teacher to pass him because he is trying. He says the teacher passes the troublemakers but punishes him. It may look this way to him since his behavior in the class is excellent.

Continue the small group discussions by pinpointing verbal clues that indicate a teacher's feelings. Some of these clues are:

Isn't it awful teaching the L.C.D.'s (lowest common denominators)?
I'm just here to collect my paycheck.
If I only had more time or fewer children to teach.
Anything goes. I like to be creative and encourage my classes to do their thing.
Quietness is next to godliness.
I'll show them who's boss...
If it weren't for me...

Obviously, these are attitudes which inhibit openness in children and erect barriers to communication, learning, and mentally healthy classrooms. Teacher cooperation can help alleviate these unhealthy attitudes and override communications barriers.

COORDINATING CURRICULUM THROUGH SUBJECT MATTER CLUSTERS

Building reading skills within each subject area is an excellent way to weave curriculum patterns that strengthen vital communication skills. Sometimes we assume that only the English teacher is responsible for helping students gain reading skills. We are all responsible for incorporating reading skill development in the subject areas we teach.

Vocabulary and reading comprehension skills are enhanced when every teacher is conscious of helping students with requisite skills to read more efficiently. If a student lags in his ability to read materials at grade level, the teacher needs to accommodate him with suitable, alternative materials which he can read and understand. Otherwise, the student is being programmed for frustration and failure.

Critical reading and thinking are indispensable to every intelligent man and woman. While many students have mastered the mechanical processes involved in reading, some miss out on comprehension, hidden implications, and writers' motives. Lead students into finding out what is being said and why. They need not wait for a love letter to learn to read between the lines and into words, or how to distinguish between denotation and connotation. Help them develop analytical reading abilities now—a real asset to strengthening comprehension skills and resisting misleading persuasion.

Six ideas can be utilized in every class: (1) Within assigned materials select difficult words and concepts for discussion and clarification. (2) Familiarize students with the content. (3) Relate the materials to known ideas through frequent use of analogies. (4) Establish a purpose for reading, so that students understand what is to be learned. (5) Provide a study sheet with questions for which students are expected to find answers. (6) Give special guided help to individual remedial readers.

Consider small group departmental meetings, where a team shares workable ways to relate reading techniques to content areas:

Learning Objectives: **Student Activities:**

Social Studies

1. To explore real life problems.
2. To build an understanding of man's relationship to cultures other than his own.
3. To place events of history in sequential perspective.
4. Reading for the main idea.
5. Reading for enjoyment as a continuing activity.

1. Investigate library materials on slums, urban renewal, environmental projects, political crises, moral issues, community problems (such as garbage pickup, street repairs, tax issues, etc.)
2. Read about ethnic groups in their native countries, their peculiarities and similarities.
3. Read about social agencies such as the Peace Corps, Job Corps, Experiment in International Living, Student Exchange programs,

Learning Objectives: **Student Activities:**

Social Studies (cont'd)

scout programs. Share this information with the class.
4. Volunteer to correspond with foreign students through pen-pal organizations.

Mathematics

1. To distinguish clearly between errors in computation and errors in reading.
2. To follow simple, written directions for working mathematical exercises, then advance to more complicated problems.
3. To learn numerical language and basic terms.
4. To learn to read graphs, maps, charts, diagrams, and tables.

1. Students can restate problems in their own words to strengthen comprehension skills.
2. Bring to the class interesting math data from multi-media resources.
3. Identify how math is related to everyday life.
4. Students can learn fundamental skills in filling out deposit and withdrawal slips; reading bank statements and credit statements, and keeping a check book account accurately.
5. Obtain road maps, floor plans, conversion tables and charts to aid in building practical reading skills.

Science

1. Following directions for scientific experiments.
2. Take notes and keep a journal of scientific investigations within the classroom.
3. Learn to systematically record results of investigations.
4. Reading for specific information.

1. Students can conduct pre-experiment discussions of new terms and directions, and use work sheets provided by the teacher.
2. Investigate biographies of famous scientists, and seek articles on recent breakthroughs in the scientific field.

Learning Objectives: Student Activities:

Science (cont'd)

5. Interpreting problems, formulas, equations, and scientific language.

   3. Consult a chart of scientific terms, signs, and symbols.
   4. Assemble a class dictionary of newly learned scientific terms.

Physical Education

1. Become familiar with newspapers and sports magazines.
2. Learn sports terminology.
3. Listen and read for facts.
4. Read aloud to project information with clarity.

   1. Discuss feature articles read, such as those on sports personalities and specialized sports.
   2. Underline unknown terms in newspaper articles relating to sports.
   3. Listen, record, and evaluate daily sports broadcasts by indicating name of event, people involved, where it took place, what happened, final scores.
   4. Prepare a 10 minute "sportscast" in written form to share aloud with classmates.

ASSURING PARENT COOPERATION: INITIATING A SEX EDUCATION PROGRAM

Because sex education information taught or discussed within a school is controversial, participation in such a program should be voluntary. Educators should seek permission from the school administration before initiating the program. Parents should have the option of excluding their children from the program. If possible, include parents, teachers, and school personnel such as counselors, librarians, nurses, and psychologists.

Sex education means more than instruction concerning the facts of sex, biological and mechanistic data. Sex education in the schools should include questions about sexual stereotypes, emotions, and human relationships as well as about petting, masturbation, and premarital sexual intercourse.

Released time could be provided from the class schedule to permit students and teachers to attend the introductory program. Parents can be invited to participate jointly with their children in a series of special programs. Attendance at evening programs is usually poor; more parents might attend during the day, especially if baby sitting services were provided at the school.

Planning a Program

1. Parents and teachers can initiate a program at a Parent Teacher's Association meeting. Parents, teachers and students will be invited to attend all sessions jointly.

2. The desired goal is to improve communication between parents and teens within a school setting.

3. Encourage parents and students to read about relations between the sexes from a suggested reading list which includes both fiction and non-fiction titles. (For related readings, see Chapter 2, pp. 37 to 38.)

4. The school librarian and the English teachers could be helpful in setting up displays and making sure that the books are available.

5. Send out an invitational flyer to parents, teachers, and students.

6. Ask the principal to designate a half day of released time from classes for the initial session for those interested participants.

7. The school counselors are frequently key persons in coordinating such a controversial program. They could introduce the filmstrip, "Sex: A Moral Dilemma for Teenagers"[1] and lead the opening session in a discussion of the ideas presented in the filmstrip.

8. Prepare a hand-out for distribution to both parents and students. Include questions for discussion. A sample list follows:

Let's Talk About Our Feelings

- There are a number of things in the filmstrip that you may never have realized were on kids' minds. Is that really the way teen-agers think in our community?

---

[1]"Sex: A Moral Dilemma for Teenagers." Two Parts (Part I: 66 frames, 14 minutes; Part II: 93 frames, 20 minutes). Pleasantville, N.Y.: Guidance Associates, 1966. Sound, color.

● What points emphasized in the film do you agree with?
● Should teen-agers be asked to accept the morality of the adult generation without question?
● Do you think that adolescents have enough maturity and experience to set up and live by their own rules?
● Are all teen-agers confused, mixed up?
  Do you think confusion is common to all teens—is it part of being a teen?
  What do you think actually changes that makes one less confused as one grows older?
  Do teens feel confused because of the times we live in?
● Teen-agers like to experiment with sex. Is this true?
  Where have teens received their information about sex? Books? Movies? Friends?
  What is their responsibility in relationships with people?
  Do you think boys try to exploit girls sexually?
  Do girls ever try to exploit boys?
  What does self-control mean?
  What does self-respect mean?
● Teen-agers are under a great deal of pressure. Is this true?
  What happens when the group wants to do something a teen doesn't want to do?
  What about the question of beginning habits of social behavior?
  What habits do teens have that cause some parents to get angry, that annoy others, that cause worry?
● How do you think adults might come to understand teens better?

9. Tape record the discussion session and prepare follow-up workshops referring to questions and concerns raised during the first session.

The cooperative honing in on sex education can provide more than an educational benefit. Bacause of the general interest in the subject, it can be an effective opening wedge in the battle against rigid views and polarized positions. It can be the first step toward better intergroup communication.

2

Helping Teens Deal with Personal and Social Problems

Everything seems to have a streak of yellow in it. In some things it is gold, and in others it is canary feathers. We are looking for gold to stimulate teens to read so that school will not be a dull place.

Many of the recommended classics, upon which so many courses of study are built, simply have no relevance for today's teens. There will not be found a likeness to *Jane Eyre* or *Don Quixote* among them. The question is "What *will* these students read?" rather than "What *should* they read according to some set curriculum?" The sensitive teacher does not forget that the young person has a life that goes on before and after school.

There are closer connections than students realize between literature and their everyday lives. Sensitizing students in human relations can come through relating literature to life.

Ashley Montagu says teaching facts to children is not enough. Integrating teaching with experiences in the significance of humanity is also vital.[1]

---

[1]Ashley Montagu, *Man's Most Dangerous Myth: The Fallacy of Race* (Cleveland: World Publishing Co., 1964), p. 357.

Often the urban teen lives in a high-pressure environment. He or she knows about pollution firsthand. He or she may have already experienced dope, prostitution, alchohol "just for kicks." He or she often lives under the constant threat of teen-age gang participation and warfare. Teens frequently choose subjects such as legalization of marijuana, civil rights, abortion, or black militancy for special library projects. If books, then, are to have relevance for these students the material must be based on "living stuff," not embalmed matter. The approach is to start at a point of student interest. Urge the students to talk about subjects before introducing books.

ESTABLISHING A DIALOGUE

The idea is to create an atmosphere for students to discuss topics to which they can easily relate. In one very relaxed classroom, the teacher initiated the practice of starting the class with a ten minute "thawing period." Students would un-wind during this time and talk about any subject they desired. The conversation was usually mellow, hip and meaningful. Gangs, getting along with parents, marriage, brothers and sisters, drugs, homosexuality, man's inhumanity to man, peace, racism, war, were all thought-provoking topics which were touched upon during the "thawing period."

Often the discussion was introduced by a student voicing his or her reaction to an article appearing in the local newspaper. Sometimes, it was a grievance expressed against a television news commentator, or an article in the school paper or in a magazine. This innovative teacher was constantly on the lookout for usable materials which she held for the days when not enough interest was sparked through student discussion.

Our breath is a paradox. In the winter when we are outdoors, we can blow on our fingers to warm them. Indoors, we blow on a spoonful of hot soup to cool it. When students establish a dialogue with the teacher, sometimes the air is hot and sometimes cool but at least the classroom is not a morgue. A humane revolution is going on. No one is proving anything, but rather each is reflecting on personal experiences and values and catching on to new ones. Many students begin to realize a good feeling of acceptance as young adults who have something to say that is worth listening to.

The enjoyment of finding out the "how and why" of people's behavior bubbles over. After the conversation and the peeling away of the onion of life to get at the core and finding no core, students are urged to read to find some answers or clarification of ideas in print.

TOPICS FOR EXPLORATION

To stimulate teens to read fact and fiction, the innovator can appear nonchalant while setting up displays of books dealing with social problems. The fact that the first books are made easily accessible will quickly introduce them. The principle is easy to understand. We seek to secure satisfactions as effortlessly as possible.

Selected books can be grouped into the following broad topics:

1. Home and Family Relations
2. Sex and Unwanted Pregnancy
3. Homosexuality
4. Divorced Parents and Step Relatives
5. Mental Retardation and Emotional Disturbance

The topics should be analyzed by emphasizing critical thinking, reading for enjoyment, and tactful discussion, and not by a boring item-by-item account of what the student has read. Teachers should avoid selecting materials with content with which they are uncomfortable. The guidance counselor or other pupil personnel worker may be invited to join in the presentation of these units.

HOME AND FAMILY RELATIONS

Understanding home and family life offers us an opportunity to understand the emotional deprivation of confined living. Many students, especially urban students, come from homes where there is no place to be alone to enjoy an individual mood, no privacy, poor communication between members of the family, fear or insecurity, and no strong adult figures for them to emulate. The teacher can use books which portray these factors in life as it is lived at a struggling level of endurance. Although students come from different economic strata in society, their home and family struggles are frequently comparable.

Suppose we observe two situations in which the teacher attempts to get his or her class off to a fresh and enthusiastic start on a discussion of books dealing with home and family life.

Case A

(What is your reaction to this approach?)

Teacher: I think we are supposed to talk about books dealing with home and family life today.

Student: What? More books to read?

Teacher: Precisely! How else do you suppose you could possibly discuss the topic intelligently? You certainly are by far the laziest class I have and, without reading, you are much too immature to know how to answer any questions properly . . .

Student: Aw, now you're beginning to sound like my mom when she gets mad at me . . .

Teacher: Sure, and she probably has every reason to get "mad," too, judging from your reactions to a simple reading assignment. Whew! One would think I was trying to get blood out of a turnip!

One of the most obvious mistakes in this example is that the teacher has already interjected a feeling of incapability in her students by informing them that they are lazy, ignorant, and too young to cope with their problems.

Case B

(Now, how would you react to this approach—if you were a student?)

Teacher: Today's teen-agers are exposed to much more intelligence than they were in the past because of the various forms of communication media. It's obvious that many are much better read and better informed, better fed and more physically fit, and certainly better equipped to cope with the stresses of today's living!

And speaking of stresses, I never really realized that teens have to cope with so many problems until I started compiling this bibliography of teen novels—which brings us to today's topic, *Home and Family Relations.*

But before we get into this discussion, suppose we start by talking about some of our teen-age home problems. How do *you* feel about your home life? Do you think it's perfect?

Student: No! Far from it.

Student: Yeah—if only my kid sister would just drown!

Student: It would be, if my ol' man would get off my back.

Student: Well, there's this girl who lives near me. She's a nice kid, but she's got so many problems it makes me really appreciate my home life.

Teacher: What kinds of problems?

Student: Like her mom's alcoholic. She has to keep house, play nurse-maid to her younger brothers and sisters, and go to school. She's real scared of her mom, too, especially when she's stoned. I really count myself lucky.

Student: My home life is not the worst, but it could stand a lot of improvement. Or maybe I should say, it could stand a lot of space 'cause our main problem I think is space. It's just too crowded. We are constantly jumping down each other's throats because we are just so close. We're practically stepping on each other's toes.

Teacher: You're telling me some *real* problems now, aren't you, that teens experience in their home and family situations? I believe that you **could** be in a better position, perhaps, than many adults to **evaluate** books depicting teens coping with some of these very issues which you have just raised. How do you feel about that? Do you think you could?

Needless to say, the class response in Case B was more positive, more enthusiastic and generated more excitement than did the response in Case A. Also, in Case B the teacher elicited interest immediately in the topic by first complimenting her students. She also indirectly confided that adults may be detached from teen problems, unless a special effort is made by them to understand their stresses, as exemplified by her statement, "I never really realized that teens have to cope with so many problems until I started to compile this bibliography of teen novels . . ."

Lastly, when she asked for student reactions, the innovative teacher was able to unravel many problems (*e.g.,* over-crowded living conditions, the generation gap, understanding sisters and brothers, parental alcoholism), many of which are treated in the following bibliography.

Suggested Readings on Home and Family Relations

Fact

Cain, Arthur H. *Young People and Parents*. New York: John Day, 1971.

Dorman, Michael. *Under 21; a Young People's Guide to Legal Rights*. New York: Delacorte Press, 1970.

Ginott, Haim. *Between Parent and Teen-ager*. New York: Macmillan, 1969.

Jenkins, Gladys and Joy Neuman. *How to Live With Parents*. Chicago: Science Research Associates, 1948.

Menninger, William C., *et al. Blueprint for Teen-age Living*. Eau Claire, Wisconsin: Hale, 1958.

Menninger, William C., *et al. How to Be a Successful Teenager*. New York: Sterling Publishing Co., 1966.

Ullman, Frances. *Getting Along With Brothers and Sisters*. Chicago: Science Research Associates, 1948.

Vermes, Hal G. *The Boy's Book of Personal Development*. New York: Association Press, 1964.

Whiteside-Taylor, Katharine. *Getting Along with Parents*. Chicago: Science Research Associates, 1952.

Fiction

Cleaver, Vera and Bill Cleaver. *Delpha Green & Company*. Philadelphia: Lippincott, 1972.

Colman, Hila. *Bride at Eighteen*. New York: William Morrow, 1966.

Corcoran, Barbara and Bradford Angier. *A Star to the North*. Camden, N.J.: Nelson, 1970.

Dickson, Marguerite. *Only Child*. New York: David McKay, 1952.

Feagles, Anita Macrea. *Me, Cassie*. New York: Dial Press, 1968.

Head, Ann. *Mr. and Mrs. Bobo Jones*. New York: Putman, 1967.

Hunt, Irene. *Up a Road Slowly*. Chicago: Follett, 1966.

Hunter, Kristin. *God Bless the Child*. New York: Scribner's, 1964.

Jackson, Jesse. *Tessie*. New York: Harper & Row, 1968.

Medearis, Mary. *Big Doc's Girl*. Philadelphia: Lippincott, 1950.

Tate, Joan, *Sam and Me*. New York: Coward-McCann, 1968.

When studying this segment, the teacher may want to read a good professional title, such as Ruth Shonle Cavan's *Marriage and Family in the Modern World; A Book of Readings*.[2] The readings will be especially useful for background information on the family in the United States. Not only will you be able to gain a historical perspective on the family from colonial times in America to the family of the future, but specific chapters can give you an accurate picture of alcoholism in the family, unemployment, family conflicts, the unsuccessful marriage, divorce and unwed parenthood. Many teens today are battling these real situations in their own home lives.

Culminating the Unit

To culminate the assignment, you may wish to tie in the home and family life of your students with those of their parents.

1. Involve students by asking them to bring in snapshots of their parents when they were teens in high school, college, technical or vocational school; pictures of their homes, their neighborhoods and cities, etc.
2. Share old clothing worn in the "day" of their parents.
3. Collect souvenirs, old newspapers stories, diaries, photo albums, scrapbooks, which could be shared with the class.
4. Activate students into setting up exhibits of these materials and writing a class story, contrasting their lives as teens with their parents' teen years. Use snapshots and mementoes brought in by members to illustrate the story.
5. Invite parents to share stories about what life was like when they were teens.

A simple invitation to parents to visit the classroom and be a part of this "sharing" period may provide an opportunity for teacher and parent to talk in an informal setting about the progress of these students. This is encouragement that both student and parent need, to pave the way for additional pleasant relationships with the school.

Frequently the parents of our students, particularly the unmotivated ones, do not feel that they can contribute anything toward their children's successes at school. "What can I do, if the

---

[2]Ruth Shonle Cavan. *Marriage and Family in the Modern World: A Book of Readings.* 3rd ed. (New York: Crowell, 1969).

teacher can't do anything to interest my child?" is a defeatist attitude voiced by many parents of unmotivated students.

A well-planned, successfully implemented unit on *Home and Family Life* should provoke increased interest in reading and establishing a triangular dialogue between students, parents and teachers.

SEX AND UNWANTED PREGNANCY

Some questions to encourage the teen-aged creators, procreators, and jubilators to think analytically about responsibility in a relationship with another person cluster around the second broad topic, *Sex and Unwanted Pregnancy*. This controversial topic can signal a lively discussion and a possibility for follow-up reading in fact and fiction. This is the first generation to grow up knowing that effective contraception has made sexual relations without having babies possible. However, knowing this information and making use of it responsibly are often different things for the student.

Sex is an important part of life. Teens are aware of their genuine need for receiving love and for expressing love. Loving may begin with a kiss and lead to sexual intercourse. It can be a powerful experience and it also can be a very confusing experience for teens. A touch, a kiss, an embrace, skin to skin nearness are symbolic gestures of certain degrees of commitment to the other person. They are also means for escaping from the despair of everyday problems.

Class discussion can begin with an analysis of nonverbal and verbal signals and symbols. The ability to process and use spoken and unspoken symbols is important. Almost any behavior or emotion can be either an honest expression or a dishonest manipulation.

Some teachers might not feel comfortable guiding the class in a discussion about the responsibilities of loving someone. However, the classroom will probably buzz with excitement if you dare to permit discussion about that sunbeam that pierces the storm—love.

For a lively beginning, try this suggestion:

Teacher: Continuing our unit on social problems facing today's teens, in our discussion today we want to freely and openly express what it means to be a young teen in today's world. Remember, the kinds of literature we will be reading and discussing in this unit will be based on "living stuff"—that is, books dealing with problems that are relevant to teens. Also, it is important for us to realize the kinds of help in problem-solving and inspiration that can be obtained from reading both fact and fiction.

Suppose we start today's discussion by asking a few questions:

1. What are some of the problems that girls and boys encounter in expressing their sexual feelings or in checking them?
2. What are some of the "unanswered" questions that seem to worry teens the most?
3. Are these questions ones which have to do with the anatomical structure of the body, like the parts of a girl's body or the parts of a boy's body, or are they questions like the following (numbers 4 through 8)?
4. How can I get Jerry to notice *me* instead of Penny? (Or Penny to notice me instead of Jerry?)
5. What can I do to *keep* him (or her) noticing me?
6. How should I act to *hold* his (or her) affections?
7. How can I keep from getting pregnant? (Or impregnating her?)
8. Should I or shouldn't I have sex before I'm married?

Once the conversation has been ignited, a dialogue can be correlated with the titles on *Sex and Unwanted Pregnancy* listed on pages 37-38. These books may be placed on display prior to the class period.

Establishing a Dialogue

In one typical discussion session, the dialogue went like this:

Teacher: Have you ever thought about what it means to be a girl? About what it means to be in love?

Girl 1:   It means having a lot of problems . . .

Girl 2:   Yeah, like if you go with a boy and you like him, well, he expects you to have sex with him. If you don't want to, most of the time he'll think about quitting you and going with somebody else who will. That's one of the main problems in being a girl.

Girl 3:   Being a girl is hard. Most of the time you try to look pretty. This usually causes the boys to look at you, then the other girls get jealous because you attract the boys.

Teacher: Okay. Let me ask you a general question: What is love to you? You know, it's been defined a lot of different ways. What do you think about love?

Girl 1: Well, I think love is caring for somebody for more reasons than one, like not just going with a boy because he's in the crowd or because he wears "tough" clothes. I think it means having a warm feeling for someone. You like to be with this special person, and you think this special person likes to be with you.

Girl 2: Love is that feeling you get when you really like a boy. He treats you like you're really someone special, and it makes you feel good.

Girl 3: I think pretty much like the others, but especially when the boy sets you aside from all the other girls and says, "This is my girl," and lets everybody know it. And when he acts nice toward you, and is aware that both of you are still young.

Girl 4: Well, I agree with the other girls in all ways, too. But, sometimes love can be blind. Because, you know, with some girls and some people—they love a person so much that they'll do anything, just to keep him and keep their love like it is. And they'll go through anything. So love is really blind in a way.

Boy 1: I really believe it's just a feeling, between the two who care the most about each other. It can only be felt between each other.

Boy 2: A lot of girls say we put pressure on them to prove their love. I would say that she has got to be kind of dumb to think that she's in love at such an early age. Really, it could be only a strong feeling. Really. She could be feeling that she's in a strain (at such an early age) that she has to be drawn toward this individual, which I really don't think is true.

Boy 3: Then most girls tend to want to blame the boys if something goes wrong. Like they would come back to the person and say, "It's your fault, what I've done and what's been going on between us, 'cause I didn't want to do it . . . It's just the way I felt about you."

Boy 4: Most grownups think that it's only "puppy love" with teen-agers. They don't really understand that at our ages we have strong feelings for each other. When I'm with a girl I'd, to be perfectly frank, really like for her to be herself—and I would like to bring out those strong feelings. I'd like to express my own strong feelings for her, like kissing and little "puppy love" stuff. But, if we're by ourselves somewhere . . . well, that's another story.

Teacher: Who does the stopping? Who's supposed to do the stopping? Is it you who does the stopping, or is it the girl's responsibility?

Boy 1: Really, we have the responsibility to stop any action brought out toward the girl. Really, it's her say-so, whether she wants to be brought out or to carry it on, or not. It's really up to her whether we should carry it on, or stop.

Boy 2: Most of the time, the boy will go as far as she'll let him. So it's up to her to put on the brakes.

As the conversation continues, some questions to spark the dialogue are:

1. Do teens have enough maturity and experience to set up and then live by their own rules?
2. What kinds of cues do you send to the opposite sex? Are they purposeful?
3. Are you ready to accept full responsibility for the outcomes which may result from sexual relationships, or from their becoming known?
4. What are your feelings about love and loving someone?
5. Where can you go to find answers to your questions about love, sex, and marriage?

The possibilities for developing this section into an interesting and challenging unit are limitless. A plan for a unit on *Sex and Unwanted Pregnancy* could have as its purpose to develop an integrated program of services to high school teachers and students which will encourage team teaching, mini-courses, independent study and extensive use of library materials.

Teachers in the following subject areas may work together: health and safety education, general science, home economics, social studies and English. The program may also involve other school personnel, such as librarians, counselors, the school nurse, social worker, and audio-visual specialists.

The following plan is suggested.

SEX AND UNWANTED PREGNANCY
I. Objectives of the Unit.
   A. Introduce students through books and non-book materials to a better understanding of sex and pregnancy and to a full realization of their responsibilities in healthy relationships with the opposite sex.
   B. Develop a scientific knowledge of the growth and development of man from a single cell.

C. Eliminate superstitions, misconceptions and "taboos" regarding the natural phenomenon of pregnancy and birth through open discussion and scientific explanations of the topic.
D. Deepen the pupils' identification with and appreciation of family traits and family living.
E. Present a scientific vocabulary to properly describe the words dealing with the subject, while teaching also the pronunciation, syllabication and meaning of each word.
F. Encourage students to seek out the use of community resources in working on classroom assignments.
G. Reinforce knowledge of basic library skills and, at the same time, introduce a variety of newer educational media in the library on the given topic.

II. Preparations for the Unit.
A. Meet with the other personnel involved. Plan procedures for readying classrooms.
B. Enumerate the types of materials needed (classroom collections, films, filmstrips, models, charts, diagrams, etc.).
C. Indicate the types of services required of the library *(e.g., library instruction, a schedule of audio-visual equipment needed, requests for reserve books, bibliographies for teachers and students).*

III. Participants' Roles in Presenting the Unit.
A. Assign specific topics to staff members. Ask them to talk informally at an introductory period on these subjects:
   1. Home Economics teacher—Introduction of Project
   2. Librarian—Tips on Library Research
   3. English and Science teachers—Learning New Words and Concepts Associated with the Topic
   4. Social Studies teacher—Exploring and Appreciating One's Identity in Family Life.
   5. Health and Safety Education teacher—Eliminating Superstitions, Misconceptions or "Taboos" Regarding Pregnancy and Birth
B. Allow students a questions and answer period following each presentation.

IV. Student's Reading
A. Encourage students to learn more about the factual and the emotional aspects of sexuality through their reading of fiction and nonfiction titles such as those listed here.

B. Their reading can serve as the basis for assignments, research or independent study projects.

C. Ask students to jot down questions they would like to raise or want clarified on the physiological aspects of reproduction, as they read the assignments.

Suggested Readings on Sex and Unwanted Pregnancy

Fact

Bauer, W. W. and Florence. *Way to Womanhood.* New York: Doubleday, 1965.

Bill, Robert R. *Premarital Sex in a Changing Society.* Englewood Cliffs, N.J.: Prentice-Hall, Inc. 1966.

Butcher, Ruth L., *et al. Teen Love, Teen Marriage.* New York: Grosset & Dunlap, 1966.

Dalrymple, Williard. *Sex Is for Real: Human Sexuality and Sexual Responsibility.* New York: McGraw-Hill, 1969.

Detweiler, Herbert J. *How to Stand Up for What You Believe.* New York: association Press, 1967.

Corman, Michael. *Under 21.* New York: Delacorte Press, 1971.

Duvall, Evelyn Millis. *About Sex and Growing Up.* New York: Association Press, 1968.

_____. *Love and the Facts of Life.* New York: Association Press, 1963.

Fiction

Craig, Margaret Maze. *It Could Happen to Anyone.* New York: T.Y. Crowell, 1961.

Eyerly, Jeannette. *A Girl Like Me.* Philadelphia: Lippincott, 1966.

Hawthorne, Nathaniel. *The Scarlet Letter.* Westminister, Md.: Modern Library.

Kamm, Josephine. *Young Mother.* New York: Duell, Sloan and Pearce, 1965.

Sherburne, Zoa. *Too Bad About the Haines Girl.* New York: William Morrow, 1967.

Stirling, Nora. *You Would If You Loved Me.* Philadelphia: Lippincott, 1969.

Zindel, Paul. *My Darling, My Hamburger.* New York: Harper & Row, 1969.

Fact

_____.*Why Wait Till Mar-
riage?* New York: As-
sociation Press, 1965.

Glassberg, G.Y. *Barron's
Teenage Sex Counselor.*
New York: Barron's
Educational Series, Inc.,
1965.

Gersh, Marvin and Iris F. Litt.
*The Handbook of
Adolescence.* New York:
Stein and Day, 1971.

Hettlinger, Richard F. *Growing Up With Sex.* New
York: Seabury Press,
1971.

Kirkendall, Lester A. *Understanding Sex.* Chicago:
Science Research As-
sociates, 1957.

Levinson, Florence. *What
Teenagers Want to Know.*
Chicago: Budlong, 1967,

Pike, James A. *Teenagers and
Sex; A Guide for Parents.*
Englewood Cliffs, N.J.:
Prentice-Hall, 1965.

V. The Use of Films and Filmstrips.
    A. Show films on sex, again encouraging students to raise ques-
       tions after the film.
    B. The following list includes filmstrips and films which have been
       quite helpful in arousing students' interest:

Filmstrips

Kidd, Paul R. *Being Responsible About Sex and Love..*
    Includes two filmstrips: "Responsible Sexual Attitudes," 52
    frames; and "Responsible Sexual Behavior," 51 frames. Family
    Films, 1966. Sound, color.
        The filmstrips in this kit are designed for school use in
    guidance programs, social health services, programs of sex
    education, family life education, etc. The purposes of the

filmstrips are to guide young people in understanding the place of sex in their lives, and to help them develop responsible attitudes and behavior in their relationships. (Running time, 11 and 10 minutes, respectively.)

Sex: A Moral Dilemma for Teenagers. Two Parts (Part I: 66 frames, 14 minutes; Part II; 93 frames, 20 minutes). Pleasantville, New York: Guidance Associates, 1966. Sound, color.

Includes a "Counselor's Guide" with an introduction to counselors for use as an audio-visual aid for guidance and group discussion. Gives introductory questions (if needed) to open group discussions. Also includes suggestions and questions for classroom discussion.

Films

About Sex. Texture Films (1600 Broadway, New York 10019), 1972. Color. 23 minutes. Study guide upon request. Preview available.

This film is a sequel to *A Three-Letter Word for Love.* It deserves wide distribution in sex education programs. The film is set in a ghetto. It stars a rock group and young people from 15 to 20 years of age. A frank discussion includes topics such as venereal disease, the sex act, masturbation, homosexuality, aphrodisiacs, abortion and birth control.

When Life Begins. Produced by Cinematheque Guigoz; Distributed by McGraw-Hill Films (1221 Avenue of the Americas, New York 10020), 1968; 1972. Preview available.

"Intended for use in biology and embryology classes, this unique film presents a sequence of events in the growth and development of the human fetus from ovulation to birth. Film shows development of individual organs as they relate to the other organ systems and to the entire fetus." (*Previews,* April, 1973, p. 19).

C. Follow the film with a period of open discussion.

D. Summarize daily activities, pointing up relationships between the reading assignment or film presentation and questions that came up during discussion periods.

E. Give specific assignments for either group or committee work, and/or independent study projects.

VI. Vocabulary

A. Have students study the following new words (spelling, syllabication, pronunciation, meaning):

1. chromosome   3. fertilization
2. Fallopian tube 4. fetus

5. gene	15. puberty
6. hormone	16. secretion
7. menstruation	17. spermatozoa
8. ovum	18. testes
9. ovary	19. umbilical cord
10. oviduct	20. uterus
11. pelvis	21. vagina
12. penis	22. vulva
13. pituitary gland	23. womb
14. placenta	

  B. Teachers and students may wish to add to this list as the assignment progresses.

V. Evaluation and Follow-Up Activities

  A. Engage students in individual projects (such as creating exhibits, displays, posters, drawings, plaster of Paris models, charts, diagrams, etc.).

  B. Encourage students to write creatively (term papers, essays, compositions, stage plays, radio scripts, etc.).

  C. Assign students to function in group or committee projects such as student forums, utilizing resource persons from the community—*e.g.,* minister, doctor, nurse, social worker—through debates or taped presentations.

  D. The teacher may evaluate the students' progress at the completion of the project through personal observation and written examination.

  E. Culminate the unit with a field trip to a nearby museum of science.

HOMOSEXUALITY

The innovative teacher realizes that this is a very "touchy" subject. However, it is a topic about which young people are naturally inquisitive. While the literature on the topic is limited, its recent treatment in factual books and novels attests to our greater understanding and acceptance of bisexuals and homosexuals. Through a discussion of this subject, students can be encouraged to accept and to try to understand individual differences.

The topic of homosexuality may be troublesome to a teacher who cannot always control a class discussion. If this is true the teacher can omit this unit. The topic may also create anxiety in parents who are fearful that discussion connotes approval and will encourage youthful experimentation.

Establishing Objectives

Allow the students in this group to set up their own objectives for evaluating the books suggested in the bibliography of this section:

Example

1. Stress the human characteristics and uniqueness of all people and the avoidance of sexual stereotypes.
2. Discuss conflicts which arise from differences in cultural norms and behavior patterns of men and women.
3. Help others discover the "preciousness" of each life.

Suggested Readings on Homosexuality

Fact

Duvall, Evelyn Millis. *Love and the Facts of Life.* New York: Association Press, 1963.

Glassberg, B.Y. *Barron's Teenage Sex Counselor.* New York: Barron's Educational Series, 1965.

Weinberg, George H. *Society and the Healthy Homosexual.* New York: St. Martin's Press, 1972. (for professional use)

Fiction

Baldwin, James. *Giovanni's Room.* New York: Dial, 1956.

Donovan, John. *I'll Get There. It Better Be Worth the Trip.* New York: Harper & Row, 1969.

Holland, Isabelle. *The Man Without a Face.* Philadelphia: Lippincott, 1972.

Samuels, Gertrude. *Run, Shelley, Run,* New York: Crowell, 1974.

Discussion Questions

1. Is the author "preaching" for or against homosexuality?
2. Who are the members of the Gay Activist Alliance?
3. What is lesbianism? hermaphroditism? (What is the source of your information?)
4. Is there any relation between the previous words and these: fag, weirdo, dyke, butch, fruit?
5. Is the homosexual experience that is related in the book between boy and boy, girl and girl, or between two adults (male or female), or one adult and one teen-ager?
6. How would you rate the experiences of the main characters in the story? Realistic_____ Distorted_____ Mediocre_____ Painful_____? Why?

7. If you were to re-write portions of the book, what sections would you choose and how would you re-write them? Defend your position.

DIVORCED PARENTS AND STEP RELATIVES

This topic can be introduced by using articles from a newspaper which carries a syndicated "Dear Abby" type column. These articles are usually written in a chatty style and easily read. Letters about love, marriage, and divorce are sometimes humorous. Through them, students may be led to understand the seriousness of personal problems and how people seek to solve them.

Sample Article

Dear Abby:

I'm tired of being in the middle in witnessing the arguments between my mom and dad. Why can't they be nice to each other? They want me to take sides and I think they both act silly and mean. They talk of divorce.

For example, yesterday my dad bought me a new bike and Mom made me take it back because she said Dad was buying my love. That started argument #395.

Help! I am so confused. What can I do to help my parents? If they divorce, who should I live with? I can't bear this alone.

Signed,

BEWILDERED

Children of divorced parents are often overwhelmed in trying to understand the "why" of the parting of the ways.

Establishing a Dialogue

The sample article can be used to establish a dialogue with students. Ask students to supply answers to the questions asked by "Bewildered." The teacher can begin the discussion with these introductory remarks:

Teacher: When Mom and Dad's conflicts meet head on, sometimes divorce results. Perhaps compromise and concession were thoroughly explored, maybe not. These are key words— compromise and concession—for understanding ways to overcome obstacles in personal relationships. Do you know the meanings of these words?

After creating an interest in the topic, place in students' proximity books and articles exploring the topic further:

Suggested Readings on Divorced Parenthood

Fact	Fiction
Cavan, Ruth Shonle. *Marriage and Family in the Modern World.* 2d ed. New York: T.Y. Crowell, 1965. (for professional use, Chapter 17)	Blume, Judy. *It's Not the End of the World.* Englewood Cliffs, N.J.: Bradbury Press, 1972.
Gardner, Richard A. *The Boys and Girls Book About Divorce.* New York: Science House, 1970.	Cavanna, Betty. *A Breath of Fresh Air.* New York: William Morrow, 1966.
Rohner, Louise. *The Divorcee's Handbook.* New York: Doubleday, 1967.	Duncan, Lois. *A Gift of Magic.* Boston: Little, Brown & Co., 1971.
	Greene, Constance G. *A Girl Called Al.* New York: Viking, 1969.
	Platt, Kin. *The Boy Who Could Make Himself Disappear.* Philadelphia: Chilton, 1968.
	Stolz, Mary S. *Leap Before You Look.* New York: Harper, 1972.

Follow-Up Activities

Use a Complete-the-Sentence form to create interest in the topic. Tell respondents there are no right or wrong answers:

1. Marriage is
2. If I ever married I'd
3. If I act on impulse right now I would
4. The future of marriage is
5. People divorce when
6. When parents get divorced, children feel
7. It is obvious to me that divorce
8. A partner in a marriage may create conflicts by
9. The conflict is resolved when
10. A happily married family is

Ask students to write a skit based on one or two specific ideas they may wish to point out about the topic. Use a story from a book for their frame of reference or actual experiences that they may be aware of. They may refer to a sample radio script from a book found in the library.

The re-marriage of divorced parents sometimes causes a child to feel unloved, unwanted and very confused about his or her relationship to step relatives. Since the child cannot understand the cause and effect relationship, he or she often feels cheated and angry. A child cannot always see the consequences of the decisions his parents have made. His world often becomes an "Alice-in-Wonderland" place, where people and things are not what they seem. Sometimes he creates a make believe world.

Suggest that the students in this group explore the following titles dealing with step relatives.

Suggested Readings on Step Relatives

Fact	Fiction
Cavan, Ruth Shonle, *Marriage and Family in the Modern World.* 3rd ed. New York: T.Y. Crowell, 1969. (for professional use. In chapter 21, pp. 574-78.)	Daringer, Helen Fern. *Step-Sister Sally.* New York: Harcourt Brace Jovanovich, 1952.
Gardner, Richard A. *The Boys and Girls Book About Divorce.* New York: Science House, 1970.	Eyerly, Jeannette. *Drop-Out.* Philadelphia: Lippincott, 1963.
	Whitney, Phyllis. *Linda's Homecoming.* New York: David McKay, 1950.
	Zindel, Paul. *My Darling, My Hamburger.* New York: Harper & Row, 1969.

MENTAL RETARDATION AND EMOTIONAL DISTURBANCE

There is often a queasy, cringing fear that a family member will be known as retarded. Learning to deal with problems and not run away from them is a sign of maturity. Potential dropouts or unmotivated students may identify with the problems of the exceptional child. Frequently they share a feeling of degradation. Assist students in building awareness of how others cope with problems and the nature of problems. The intent is to bring about a change of attitudes.

Establishing a Dialogue

Sometimes siblings may find a mentally retarded brother or sister difficult to accept. The mentally retarded child may feel rejected by others and may reflect this attitude in rejection of self.

Let students in this group select a representative chapter, one which is not too lengthy, from one of the titles listed under the following Suggested Readings. They may divide the chapter among themselves to read sections aloud to the class, or they may dramatize the chapter selected.

Example

Reynolds, Pamela. *A Different Kind of Sister.* New York: Lothrop, Lee and Shepard Co., Inc., 1968. (pp. 137-144)

In this story, about a teenager's rejection of her mentally retarded sister, Chapter 12 provides an excellent section for creating interest in the book. The chapter provides a dramatic incident in which Sally's retarded sister, Debbie, breaks her sister's cherished horses of white china. In the dialogue which follows, Sally bitterly exclaims to her mother, "she's spoiled everything for me—this whole summer . . . Someone like her should be in an institution. I wish she'd go back to Ferndale and stay there" (p. 142). Shortly afterwards, Debbie runs away in an apparent attempt to return to Ferndale.

For whatever title is selected, be sure that there is an ample supply of books on hand.

Suggested Readings on Mental Retardation and Emotional Disturbance

Fact	Fiction
Buck, Pearl S. *A Community Success Story; the Founding of the Pearl Buck Center.* New York: John Day Books, 1972. Also, write to: National Association for Mental Health 1800 N. Kemp Street	Brown, Roy. *Escape the River.* New York: Seabury Press, 1972. (Mental Retardation) Friis-Baastad, Babis. *Don't Take Teddy.* New York: Scribner, 1967. (Mental Retardation)

Fact	Fiction
Roselyn, Virginia 22209	Green, Hannah. *I Never Promised You A Rose Garden*. New York: Holt, 1964. (Mental Illness)
National Association for Retarded Children 2709 Avenue "E" East Arlingron, Texas 76112	Keyes, Daniel. *Flowers for Algernon*. New York: Harcourt Brace Jovanovich, 1966. (Mental Retardation)
	Platt, Kin. *Chloris and the Creeps*. Philadelphia: Chilton, 1972. (Mental Retardation)
	_____. *The Boy Who Could Make Himself Disappear*. Philadelphia: Chilton, 1968. (Emotional Disturbance)
	Reynolds, Pamela. *A Different Kind of Sister*. New York: Lothrop, Lee & Shepard Co., 1968. (Mental Retardation)
	Sherburne, Zoa. *A Stranger in the House*. New York: William Morrow, 1963. (Emotional Disturbance)
	Snyder, Zilpha Keatley. *The Witches of Worm*. New York: Atheneum, 1972. (Emotional Disturbance)

Discussion Questions

1. Discuss the concept of rejection.
2. How do you think it feels to be perceived by the group as different?
3. Why do you suppose a rejected person frequently copes with the problem by hostility? Illustrate this progression in a story:
   a. He is in the group, but not of it.

    b. He lacks friends, is lonely, becomes jealous.

    c. He seeks attention to compensate for this feeling.

4. What is meant by demoralization?

5. Constant comparison to others creates what kinds of feelings?

6. What academic standards have your parents set for you?

3

Understanding and Respecting Others

A teen-ager's world is gradually changing from make believe to real. His world is like a kaleidoscope. Things are not always as they seem, and the patterns that are viewed by some as brave acts may be seen as contemptible license by others. Sometimes conditions create problems for us; other times, joys. The teacher who is consistent and positive can help young people realize that life's problems and disappointments are concomitant with its opportunities and satisfactions.

Human relations are the basis for all other satisfactions. Besides those intimate social and family relationships already discussed, teens must learn to relate positively to those who may be different from themselves in background, appearance, or temperament.

In an integrated classroom environment, students often find themselves self-conscious about their difference instead of being proud of their place in the human race. Five activities which the innovator may implement to involve ethnic-oriented perspectives are pictured on the "Kaleidoscope of Human Relations in the Classroom" (see page 49). The teacher should keep in mind three main objectives in unraveling these activities:

1. Stress the universals, the basic similarities in life as it is lived at many different levels and under different conditions in an attempt to better understand ourselves and our great, funky American country.
2. Develop a sensitivity to the problems of people living under conditions different from one's own and reveal the stake each of us has in the plight of others, especially the disadvantaged.
3. Emphasize black, Spanish, and multi-ethnic contributions to the community.

Thinking is a difficult burden for some students, yet they need to be encouraged to formulate ideas. Don't give up. For a change, students can follow a line of interest while sitting in a classroom instead of having to follow deadlines for required readings.

THE KALEIDOSCOPE OF HUMAN RELATIONS
IN THE CLASSROOM

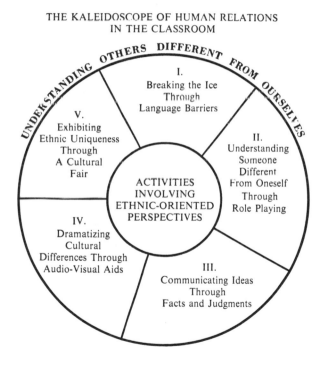

BREAKING THROUGH LANGUAGE BARRIERS

Many teachers have wanted to bridge the gap between ethnic groups in the school, and more particularly in the classroom, but have not known exactly how to go about doing it. How does a teacher break the ice when language barriers seem to create obstacles rather than encourage respect for ethnic differences?

One way is to open a discussion about physical differences. Here, the innovative teacher has a hidden agenda: To point out word choices that create barriers and learned prejudices which need to be overcome.

Establishing a Dialogue

A teacher could begin the class dialogue to help students analyze ideas which lock in stereotypes by using the following discussion:

Teacher: Outward characteristics of physique seem to reflect to many people the inner nature of man. Let's take the characteristic of blindness, for example. Blindness in the United States is defined on the basis of inability to perceive motion at a distance of one foot or Snellen Chart performance of 20/200. Yet, these same characteristics bear different connotations in different parts of the world.

Modern Turkey recognizes the blind as indispensable assets to religious ceremonies and funerals.[1] In Greek history, the blind are often referred to as clairvoyants.[2] Among the Koreans, the blind are held in high esteem because they are thought to have acquired an inner vision. The blind are often anormalized in the United States because other individuals look on them as being different.

A preconceived idea that "the blind" are helpless is difficult to change in people. There is no evidence that certain personality characteristics should be presumed as belonging to any unique group. Most of us acquire our attitudes on the significance of things by how adults and friends whom we respect react to them. A person becomes exceptional or different not only because of his real differences but also because of society's stigma and attitudes toward him.

Like a shooting star falling out of orbit while all the others continue in their accustomed rounds, the person

---

[1]Edward Maisel, *Meet a Body* (Unpublished Manuscript. Institute for the Crippled and Disabled, 1953).

[2]H. Von Hentig, *The Criminal and His Victim* (New Haven, Conn.: Yale University Press, 1948).

who feels different becomes an outcast, sometimes of his own making. Exclusion, dependency, inferiority—these attitudes characterize the problems he has to face. Individuals wish to be judged in their own right and not known by their membership in a group.

Another idea is to dramatize myths and jokes related to different ethnic groups. Students may be encouraged to write these and discuss with schoolmates the fallacious, stereotyped thinking which they represent.

All students have strengths which can be fired up. Stress the positives whenever possible. Set reachable goals so that the student feels immediate rewards.

Sometimes we overlook the talents of our bilingual students. They are often struggling between two cultures which are not quite assimilated. They sometimes feel "different." Encourage them to express their skill with pride. For example, a fourteen year old Puerto Rican girl was asked to translate the following from Aesop's *Fables* into Spanish:

THE BALD MAN AND THE FLY[3]

English	Spanish
There was once a Bald Man who sat down after work on a hot summer's day. A fly came up and kept buzzing about his bald pate, and stinging him from time to time. The man aimed a blow at his little enemy, but—whack—his palm came on his head instead; again the Fly tormented him, but this time the Man was wiser and said:	Había una vez un hombre calvo que se sento despirés de trabajar en un diá de verano caluroso. Una mosca vino volando abrededor de su cabeza calva, Picándolo devez en cuando. El hombre trat ó de dar un golpe a su pequeno enemigo, pero cuás, en vez de esto se pego en la cabeza; otra vez la mosca lo a tormentó, pero esta vez el hombre fué mas sabio y dijo:
"You will only injure yourself if you take notice of despicable enemies."	*"Si to fijas en enemigos despreciables solamente vas a lastimarte a ti mismo."*
	Translated by
	Nilsa Agosto,
	grade 9

---

[3]Aesop, *The Fables of Aesop;* Selected, Told Anew and Their History Traced by Joseph Jacobs (New York: Macmillan Co., 1964), p. 11.

This class assignment can aid young children of family friends who can only speak and understand Spanish.

This same approach can be applied to translations of jokes and riddles, folktales, fairy tales, short stories, biographies of contemporary Spanish-speaking Americans, or books of poetry. A teacher's suggestion and encouragement can lead to a meaningful activity and build motivation for learning. It can also serve as "holding power" for unmotivated students to complete a high school education.

UNDERSTANDING SOMEONE DIFFERENT FROM ONESELF THROUGH ROLE PLAYING

"Walk a while in my shoes." Understanding someone different from oneself sometimes means standing in his shoes, reflecting on his culture and his pressures in life as well as his joys. As a tuning fork will set off a sympathetic piano wire across the room, so may a teacher turn on students to begin to understand people who are different from themselves.

One way to begin this process is by encouraging role playing. Students should be seen and heard as much as possible. Classroom participation should create interest and involvement. Sometimes students who have difficulty in expressing themselves in writing perform much better in oral activities.

Members of the class may act out parts based on the book *Shadi*,[4] a story about a Navajo girl's problem in finding a comfortable place outside of the Navajo culture within the white community.

    1. The following roles may be assumed:

        Role A. You are a young missionary teacher living on an Indian Reservation. You have a positive attitude that with Indian children lies hope: that education will be "caught" by their elders. You believe America has a stake in the Indian's future.

        Role B. You are Shadi, a confused Indian teen faced with the problems of growing up and also relating to the world apart from the Navajos.

[4]Margaret Embry, *Shadi* (New York: Holiday House, 1971.)

You feel guilty about being away from family
responsibilities during the day.

Role C. You are Shadi's father who is responsible for
seven children, drinks heavily and is not sure
that the education of the "white man" is what
he wants for his daughter.

2. Set the tone by discussing the characters and their choices.
What kind of a person do you think would take the job of
a missionary teacher on an Indian reservation?
Why do you think some Indians distrusted her? What
special concerns faced the Indians?

3. Tape record the role playing. Indicate that while listening
to voices students should remember facial cues about feelings.

4. Play back the tape and, through class discussion, interpret
the roles.

   a. Discuss how people find themselves set apart from
   others because of the way they feel, their physical
   characteristics, social status, language barriers,
   customs.

   b. Emphasize the aspects of justice versus injustice and
   individual choice versus conformity to a prevailing
   culture as ever-present problems of the human race.

   c. Zero in on the special conflicts in each role. The missionary teacher, for example, is attempting to
   motivate Shadi to come to school to learn how to
   function in the world in a way that is different from
   the way that her parents did.
   At the same time, the teacher is trying to gain the
   trust of the girl's parents.

Similar role playing situations can be developed from many
of the novels listed under Suggested Readings for this topic. Plan
questions, projects and activities designed to relate the concepts
discussed in this unit to typical life situations.

COMMUNICATING IDEAS THROUGH
FACTS AND JUDGMENTS

How we see things is often determined by how we have been
taught to respond to certain cues. The innovative teacher can

build an awareness of the difference between facts and judgments by introducing this lesson.

Begin by reading the tale of "Custer's Last Stand" as recorded in students' history texts. Then present the picture story as seen through the eyes of a 15-year old Sioux Indian boy in the book, *Red Hawk's Account of Custer's Last Battle*.[5] Since this is a picture story, you may wish to use the opaque projector to illustrate and counterpoint ideas presented by the Indian lad and the text historian.

Notice that this lesson encourages class participation by asking students to use analytical skills. Students are instructed to point out differences in interpretation of an historic event, depending upon whose side they favored. No one has to be an authority; each can speak from his own frame of reference. Encourage students to discuss myths about the American Indian. With what inequities has the Indian been confronted? Ask students to tabulate which thoughts seem to be facts and which judgments, and create in them a determination not to willfully confuse the two.

Follow-Up Ideas

To strengthen students' perceptions about the differences between facts and judgments about people, ask them to bring to class colorful pictures from magazines or newspapers that show men, women and children from different ethnic and cultural backgrounds.

1. Ask students to mark off their paper into two columns: one for facts, one for judgments.
2. Flash each picture on the overhead projector and ask the class to list facts about what the face indicates. Then list judgments: Does this seem like someone you would like? Is he or she of a different race? Is he or she of lower status or higher status?
3. Discuss nonverbal cues, such as signs of friendship (a smile, a friendly look, a touch). Then discuss signs of fear or hostility (a frown, a glare, a jerking away).
4. Let a student leader pull together the lists of facts and judgments for each picture. Sum these up and post them under the pictures which can then be displayed on a bulletin board after the lesson.

---

[5]Paul and Dorothy Goble, *Red Hawk's Account of Custer's Last Battle* (New York: Pantheon Books, 1969).

DRAMATIZING CULTURAL DIFFERENCES THROUGH AUDIO-VISUAL AIDS

"All animals are equal, but some animals are more equal than others." George Orwell in *Animal Farm*[6] hit.upon the paradoxical theme of racial inequality. Discuss how racial inequality provided an important impetus for one of the great contributions of Black Americans to this country—musical inspiration.

A unit emphasizing the unique contribution to modern music of the American Negro and ending up with the treatment of Blacks in novels could create an impetus for white students as well as Blacks to become interested in learning. You might begin with a study of jazz.

A. Discuss the Black's contribution to American jazz music.
   1. Play Leonard Bernstein's record, "What is Jazz?"[7] Emphasize how important it is that students listen for information.
   2. Encourage outside reading on the subject of jazz and jazz musicians in an attempt to have students gather material from outside classroom sources.
      a. *Current Biography*[8] is a good source for articles on popular musicians, especially since the articles are brief and interesting.
      b. Jackets of record albums also provide brief and easily-read data. Also, students enjoy bringing their favorite records to school.
      c. Introduce vocabulary dealing with jazz: improvisation, downbeat, blue notes, harmony, minor and major keys, traditional, progressive.
   3. Stress the significance of jazz in the field of music.
B. Discuss gospel music. Consider how Negro spirituals influenced music of other cultures.
   1. Offer recorded samples of the music of Mahalia Jackson, for example.
   2. Suggest background readings on gospel music.

---

[6]George Orwell, *Animal Farm* (New York, N.Y.: Harcourt Brace Jovanovich, Inc., 1954).

[7]Leonard Bernstein, *What Is Jazz?* Columbia, 12" 33⅓ rpm.

[8]*Current Biography* (New York: H.W. Wilson, 1940-present).

C. Discuss how folk music reflects the suffering as well as the celebration of a people, *e.g.* songs of the chain gang, wedding songs, play and dance tunes.
D. Play selections from records of ethnic groups such as Polish, Greek, Indian, Chinese.
   1. Discuss how we react to sounds to which we are not accustomed.
   2. Draw analogies to how we react to people to whom we are not accustomed.
E. Analyze the contributions of other countries to our culture.
F. Play parts of "My Fair Lady"[9] to emphasize dialects and language barriers.

EXHIBITING ETHNIC UNIQUENESS THROUGH A CULTURAL FAIR

A cultural fair is fun to organize. Advertise the fair several months in advance. Invite all departments to participate and send a communication home to parents for help and participation. Invite all classes and school clubs to set up exhibits. Sometimes special ideas are helpful to get classes motivated to participate. Send a memo listing possible exhibit ideas like these:

- Pattern clay models of life in other countries.
- Draw a poster indicating a battleground with an accompanying report explaining what nations sometimes fight about.
- Arrange a fashion show to exhibit styles from different cultures.
- Set up picture displays indicating ethnic types, scenes from other societies.
- Teach ethnic dances and arrange a program with a special human relations theme.
- Coordinate a Tasting Party of foods from different cultures.
- Let foreign language students arrange a musical program featuring songs in French and Spanish.
- Invite parents to set up displays of products made in other countries.
- Let parents sponsor a bake sale of cakes and pastries.
- Display dolls from different nations.

---

[9]*My Fair Lady;* Rex Harrison and Julie Andrews with Stanley Holloway. Columbia, OL 5050. 12" 33 ⅓ rpm.

- Explore life in other countries today. Write summaries with graphs, pictures, maps.
- Create a mural in memory of a favorite national hero or heroine.

UNDERSTANDING OTHERS THROUGH LITERATURE

The innovative teacher will also find that a unit on "Fact and Fiction" will provide an excellent medium for increasing students' understanding of human differences.

1. Introduce a unit stressing novels dealing with a racial or cultural conflict such as that of the American Negro in white society. Notice the list of sources included in this chapter under Suggested Readings.
2. Encourage students to realize that our American society is only one of a great variety of possible social structures. What elements of society should be modified or rejected?
3. Place books with ethnic-oriented plots within students reach. Encourage browsing, which hopefully leads to reading.

Setting The Stage

To get students to zero in on particulars of novels and to read meaningfully, consider these suggestions for helping them pinpoint ideas:

1. Place the book in its proper setting: Designate the time, period, era, geographical location.
2. Who are the characters? Does the author portray characters realistically? Do they differ from each other? React to their character traits. Do you know any persons who remind you of the characters in the novel? Are the characters introduced through dialogue? By way of narrative descriptions? Discuss how the characters changed because of their experiences. (For example, did they begin to trust people more, distrust them, become withdrawn, or take charge of the situations? Relate the social pressures the main character had to face to those that other people face.)
3. Upon what social problem, if any, is the book built? (If a student does not choose to read a book dealing with a social problem, he should still be encouraged to read something that interests him.)
4. What significant incidents occurred because of the reaction of a person or persons to a stress situation?

5. Were you able to predict what the outcome of the story would be before the final chapter?

6. Did you agree or disagree with the outcome of the story? Why?

7. If you were to rewrite the final chapter, how would you change the ending? Why?

8. What are your own personal comments, criticisms, suggestions about this book?

Suggested Readings For Understanding Others Through Literature

Fact

Alexander, Rae Pace and Julius Lester. *What It Means to be Young and Black in America.* New York: Random House, 1970.

Blain, Graham B. Jr. *Youth and Hazards of Affluence.* New York: Harper & Row, 1966.

Brooks, Charlott, ed. *The Outnumbered.* New York: Delacorte, 1969.
A collection of stories, essays and poems about minority groups.

David, Jay, ed. *Growing Up Black.* New York: William Morrow, 1968.

Drotning, Phillip and Wesley South. *Up From the Ghetto.* New York: Cowles Book Co., 1970. "The inspiring stories of some ghetto blacks who really wanted to make it big—and did." (Cover)

Floyd, Thomas W. *Integration Is a Bitch.* Gary, Indiana: Opinion News Syndicate, Inc., 1969.

Fiction

Bartusis, Constance. *Shades of Difference.* New York: St. Martin's Press, 1968.

Bell, Margaret E. *The Totem Casts a Shadow.* New York: Morrow, 1947.
A young white boy marries an Indian girl and is disowned by his father.

Bennett, Jay. *Masks.* New York: Franklin Watts, 1971.
Jennifer's parents had always taught her to hate prejudice until she fell in love with Peter Chen, a Chinese doctor's son.

Blackburn, Thomas Wakefield. *A Good Day to Die.* New York: David McKay, 1967.
A story of Indian life.

Butler, Beverly. *Light a Single Candle.* New York: Dodd, Mead & Co., 1962.
Teen-aged Cathy forges ahead with her leader dog, Tracey, and makes a way for herself despite her blindness.

Fact

A book of cartoons depicting many common stereotypes in black-white relations. An accompanying filmstrip by the same title is also available.

Frank, Anne. *Anne Frank; The Diary of a Young Girl.* New York: Doubleday, 1952.

Gregory, Susan. *Hey, White Girl.* New York: Norton, 1970.
A teen-aged white girl writes about her experiences in an all black high school on Chicago's South Side.

Gridley, Marion. *Contemporary American Indian Leaders.* New York: Dodd, Mead & Co., 1972.
Presents twenty-six biographies of contemporary Indian Leaders in a variety of vocations.

Griffin, John H. *Black Like Me.* Boston: Houghton Mifflin, 1960.
The author relates his experience with prejudice and injustice after he darkened his skin and spent five weeks in the South as a black man.

Halsell, Grace. *Soul Sister.* New York: World, 1969.
A white woman darkens her skin and mas-

Fiction

Butters, Dorothy Gilman. *Heartbreak Street.* Philadelphia: MaCrae Smith Co., 1958.
Seventeen-year-old Kitty Boscz learns that Pearl Street, her neighborhood and ramshackle home is only a state of mind as she gropes for maturity.

Cavanna, Betty. *Jenni Kimura.* New York: Morrow, 1964.
Jenni visits her grandmother in America, from her Indian homeland.

Colman, Hila. *Classmates by Request.* New York: Morrow, 1964.
A black girl and a white girl find themselves caught up in integration problems in a northern high school.

Crane, Caroline. *Don't Look at Me That Way.* New York: Random House, 1970.
Rosa breaks away from the stereotype of "Puerto Rican chick" to make choices that lead to a fulfilling life.

De Angeli, Marguerite. *Bright April.* New York: Doubleday, 1946.
A Negro girl joins a Girl Scout troop.

De Leeuw, Adela. *The Barred Road.* New York: Macmillan Co., 1964.
The town's prejudice is

Fact	**Fiction**
querades as black in the South.	tested by the friendship between a white girl and a black girl.
Heuman, William. *Famous American Indians.* New York: Dodd, Mead & Co., 1972.	Doss, Helen. *The Family Nobody Wanted.* Boston: Little, Brown & Co., 1954.
Includes the lives of nine well known Indians: Joseph Brant, Chief Joseph, Crazy Horse, King Philip, Osceola, Pontiac, Sequoyah, Sitting Bull and Tecumseh.	A humanistic, candid story of the adoption of children from many different nations by a Methodist minister and his wife.
Mayerson, Charlotte L., ed. *Two Blocks Apart.* New York: Holt, Rinehart and Winston, 1965.	De Trevino, Elizabeth B. *I, Juan de Pareja.* New York: Farrar, Straus & Giroux, Inc., 1965.
A Puerto Rican boy and an Irish boy express separate viewpoints about life in New York City. Both are seventeen-year-olds.	The story of Velasquez, the Spanish painter, and his Negro slave who was also an accomplished artist.
Newlon, Clarke. *Famous Mexican-Americans.* New York: Dodd, Mead & Co., 1972.	Embry, Margaret Jacob. *Shadi.* New York: Holiday House, 1971.
Include life stories of Cesar Chavez, Henry Ramirez, Joe Kapp, Joseph Montoya, Lee Trevino, and other successful Mexican Americans.	The eldest of seven Indian children is confused between choices she must make between Navajo ways and white man's ways. Her problems are compounded as she struggles with adolescence.
Sayers, Gale. *I Am Third.* New York: Viking Press, 1970.	Fredericksen, Hazel. *He-Who-Runs-Far.* New York: Young Scott Books, 1970.
An insightful story about a great black athlete who overcomes many handicaps in pursuing his goals in life.	Pablo is a part of two cultures, the Indian and white man's worlds. How he assimilates them

Fact

Terzian, James P. and Kathryn Cramer. *Mighty Hard Road; the Story of Cesar Chavez.* New York: Doubleday, 1970.
Describes an outstanding Mexican American leader's efforts to bring better living conditions, increased wages, and the unionization of workers in the California vineyards.

Thomas, Piri. *Down These Mean Streets.* New York: Alfred A. Knopf, 1967.
A vivid description of crime in the streets of Harlem.

Fiction

creates a story full of pathos.

Garfield, James B. *Follow My Leader.* New York: Viking, 1957.
A story of blindness and the "leader" dog.

Gault, William Campbell. *Drag Strip.* New York: Dutton, 1959.

Goble, Paul and Dorothy. *Red Hawk's Account of Custer's Last Battle.* New York: Pantheon Books, 1969.
Through the eyes of a fifteen-year-old Sioux Indian boy we gain a fresh perspective of "Custer's Last Stand" in a picture story.

Hentoff, Nat. *I'm Really Dragged But Nothing Gets Me Down.* New York: Simon & Shuster, 1968.
Provides a picture of a middle-class teenager's problems, among them high school matriculation, the draft and "generation gap."

Hill, Margaret. *Time to Quit Running.* New York: Messner, 1970.
A teen-aged girl finally stops "running" and discovers that she can be accepted as she is.

Hinton, S.E. *The Outsiders.* New York: Viking, 1967.
Reveals the ins and outs of a teenage gang.

Fiction

Hunter, Kristin. *The Soul Brothers and Sister Lou.* New York: Scribner, 1968.
A sophisticated novel about the life of a black family in a Northern city.

Jackson, Jesse. *Call Me Charley.* New York: Harper & Row, 1945.
The story of a young Negro boy struggling for understanding as the only black in the junior high school.

Laklan, Carli. *Migrant Girl.* New York: McGraw Hill, 1970.
Emphasizes the friendship between Dacey, daughter of a migrant family and Juan, a young Mexican-American, who are two young people of different cultural backgrounds.

Laurents, Arthur. *West Side Story.* New York: Random, 1958.
A modern version of Romeo and Juliet.

McCord, Jean. *Bitter is the Hawk's Path.* New York: Atheneum, 1971.
Ten short stories dealing with adolescent problems.

O'Dell, Scott. *Sing Down the Moon.* Boston: Houghton Mifflin, 1970.
Bright Morning, a young

Fiction

Navajo Indian girl relates in first person narrative the 300 mile journey of the Navajos in "The Long Walk to Fort Sumner" in 1864.

Randall, Florence Engel. *The Almost Year.* New York: Atheneum, 1971.

Upon her mother's death, Laurie, a black girl, is sent off to spend from September to June with a white family in a wealthy suburb.

Ramond, Charles. *Enoch.* Boston: Houghton Mifflin Co., 1969.

Growing up in the flats, a black ghetto, is a provoking experience for Enoch Parnell who is a white boy. He aligns himself with black agemates who help him bridge the racial gap and teach him the art of survival.

Steinbeck, John. *The Grapes of Wrath.* New York: Viking, 1972.

The story of migratory workers struggling to find themselves in California, as depicted through the life of the Joad family.

Underwood, Betty. *The Tamarack Tree.* Boston: Houghton Mifflin Co., 1971.

Like a balloon held

Fiction

under water, Bernadette Savard felt the pressure of the 19th century society that did not recognize women's talents. She breaks through racial barriers by having a black friend and social barriers by pursuing her interests.

Wier, Ester. *The Loner.* New York: David McKay, 1963.

A tender story about a young migratory worker's adjustment after his only friend was killed by a farm machine.

Wojciechowska, Maia. *Shadow of a Bull.* New York: Atheneum, 1964.

Manolo is expected to follow in his father's footsteps and become a bullfighter, but it is against his own wishes.

Young,Bob and Jan Young. *Across the Tracks.* New York: Messner, 1958.

A Mexican girl is the object of racial discrimination in her high school.

Follow-Up Activities

For additional assignments, zoom in on lively activities that motivate students to keep an open mind while exploring social problems:

1. Generate interest in reading fact and fiction about social problems through eye-catching displays, posters, drawings, dioramas whipped up by students themselves.

2. Encourage students to draw pictures illustrating incidents which they feel are worth sharing—from the beginning of the book, the middle, and the final chapter. Share these with class members. The stress is on feeling and recalling events, not on the art work.

   a. Help students write book summaries to go with their pictures.

   b. Gather these book summaries and pictures and put them in a booklet, so students can see their names in print.

3. Jar students to activity through a class publication dealing with books they have read. Ask them to rate each book on a scale ranging from high praise to low interest based upon their idioms:

   "Really dig it"—excellent in every way

   "Too much"—controversial

   "Tough"—good and relevant

   "All right"—fair but nothing special

   "Not together"—poor, not recommended

   When interest is really at a high level, students will produce reports like the one on page 67.

4. Check television listings for stories related to social problems. Encourage listening and discuss the program the following day.

5. Use the tape recorder to record discussion. Later ask students to write some statements in their own words. (The word is being transferred to paper.) Also, if taped discussions are good, share them with other classes. If students are asked to share their opinions, they sense that what they say is valuable. That builds confidence in themselves.

6. Sponsor a literary Coketail Party, a book fair, or an author's autograph party featuring a regional author or local journalist to talk informally with students about expressing ideas in print. Serve colas and chips as refreshments. Sometimes local bookstores or newspaper publishers will underwrite the costs of such a program.

The plan for holding teens' interest in developing a unit on *Respecting Others Different From Oneself* can be expanded to encourage not only team teaching, but also flexible scheduling, independent study, and extensive use of the library.

The teaching strategy can help students deal with questions of values, questions of personal integrity, and the great issues of human survival. We must count on communication skills to do this. Become aware of cues that lead to dialogue. Knowledge of and respect for the students' cultural backgrounds, life styles, and language helps build an awareness of another person's viewpoint on life.

UNDERSTANDING OTHERS THROUGH FOLK MUSIC

Discover how people express their culture through music. An interesting prologue to the serious study of world cultures, folk music can provide the basis for a stimulating and entertaining unit on understanding others.

Music is a source of entertainment, relaxation and enjoyment to people the world over. From ancient times to the present, man has expressed his history, his feelings, his aspirations and fears, through music. Since folk music evolves from man's daily life, all countries have their own folk songs which reflect their native language and customs.

Folk music can be divided into the following types: (1) Dance songs—the oldest type, which are an accompaniment for dancing (2) Legendary folk songs—which are usually historical or emotional narratives characterized by poetry, and (3) Composed folk songs—which generally have known composers and were written more recently than the former two types. Two well-known examples of composed folk songs are the Scottish tune "Annie Laurie" and the American song "Swanee River."

In folk music, many ingredients have remained unscathed by time and changing mores. There is still the beat of tom toms in music from Africa or the Caribbean islands. The bagpipe immediately brings to mind peasant life in Scotland and Ireland. The castanets remind the listener of Spain and Latin America. The tambourine and the lively trills and runs remind us of gypsy life in Europe. And the slow, heart-rending spirituals of the American Negro turn our thoughts to slavery in the United States.

FOLK DANCES

An interesting correlation to folk songs can be made through folk dances. A magical creation, folk dances add a special dimension that comes from sharing feelings and experiences. Folk dances symbolize the spirit of living life intensely. The dances come from ancient times and reflect religious feelings, expressions

D O N ' T   L O O K   A T   M E
T H A T   W A Y

by Caroline Crane
(New York: Random House,
1970)

(Illustration sketched from book jacket)

Rosa Rivera, a Puerto Rican, was fed up with people and their ideas. Everyone thought Latins were passionate, thieves, and dirty. No one wanted to have anything to do with them.

Rosa lived in the slums with her mother and many brothers and sisters. She had to quit school and work. She didn't like it, but someone had to support her family.

Read and see Rosa's ups and downs, feel her highs and lows, and live a part of her life. Read this book and see why she says:

"DON'T LOOK AT ME THAT WAY."

--Reviewed by Michelle Hudson, grade 9.

A Student's Report

of love, celebration of social events, and in some cases, even preparation for war.

Understanding cultures different from our own includes delving into folkways which reflect the heritage of a country. Since teens frequently enjoy dance, a social studies teacher can encourage teens to begin their search through a country's folkways with dance. Students lucky enough to live in a community with active ethnic groups can, on occasion, see people joining in the ancient dances at ethnic gatherings such as cultural affairs or programs, or simply at church picnics. Through folk dances—their expression and movement and musical rhythm—we find threads linking them with ancient texts, poetic meters, vase paintings of past cultures.

Sometimes dancers join hands or arms in an unbroken circle indicating closeness, affection, warmth, security—togetherness. Sometimes dancers separately respond to rhythms even so far as to keep men in different ritualistic dances from the women's.

A language arts teacher can use the theme of dance to freshen students' interest in the subject matter of writing assignments. Students can explore how freedom, pride and noble competition are expressed through the gestures, poses, and combinations of movements in dance. Compare popular names of dances—"the monkey," "the horse," "the bunny hop"—to the ancient names of dances such as "Kalamatianos," a coastline city in Greece and the name of a popular folk dance. Elements such as rain dancing or special occasion names such as "the wedding dance" are interesting focal points for discussion in prose and poetry.

Follow-Up Recreational Activities

Many activities which can be implemented by students themselves for their enjoyment will aid them in understanding others:

1. While playing records of folk songs, use an opaque projector to flash pictures of people from the country about which the song was written.
2. When visiting a foreign country or an ethnic event, tape songs or music heard. Share these tapes with classmates.
3. Draw pictures, or make posters or collages to depict folk singers. Do you think the picture on page 69, drawn by a 7th grader, will be considered that of a folk singer 25 years hence?

Illustrator Unknown

4. Give a multi-ethnic talent show at your school. Ask each participant or group to select a narrator to explain something about
   the music of the country that is represented.
5. Write a poem on folk dancing, or find some that others have
   written. Learn the meanings of the words that are unfamiliar.

Folkdance

I want to dance, to circle the world with hands clasping one after
another after another

To hear the kolo rhythm repeating in quickened pace, the body
straight and rigid, puppet legs and feet shuffling in unison—

increasing in speed as a bubbling pudding comes to full boil

I want to feel the pull and sway like seaweed anchored by unseen
roots in churning waters under moon tides.

To lean in strong arms, shoulder muscles bracing, feet lifting in
lightning steps while blurred faces pass like windows in a subway
tunnel.

I want to schottish like a wind-up toy, polka like a wild hare
delighting in tall clover.

I want to skip - hands pairing down a contra line, hair loose with
clapping ringing in the ears, roller coaster dizzy, bumper car happy.

I want to celebrate the movement of muscle and bone, ribs and
knees, of gazelle legs in pursuit over orange plains.

Come, dance too! Let's grasp, whirl, hang on, kick and leap, hold
together tightly, weaving our circle over the hill.

Sandra G. Olansky

4

Accentuating Career Information

Every teacher is responsible for making a real effort to help students enter the economic world without meeting overwhelming discouragement. Most teachers realize that there is a great need to expose students to accurate, up-to-date career information in each classroom, and that career information should enhance the regular educational program rather than supplant it. Exciting, career-oriented classroom activities can make students aware of job options and encourage them to take advantage of all available opportunities to prepare for these jobs.

Students should be made to feel that the schools are not requiring them to "cram" isolated facts and figures. When career activities are correlated with school activities, students will come to realize that the mastery of these skills in school can lead to their use in related careers in the future.

For example, when studying mathematics, the student will learn about career possibilities for business management in entry jobs such as salesclerk, bartender, waitress, cashier, and later jobs in personnel management, marketing, retailing, banking and finance, drafting and architecture. English teachers may demonstrate that proficiency in language arts may subsequently lead to an entry career as a telephone operator, library aide, receptionist, and to later careers in acting, advertising, education, law, library science, linguistics, office work, printing and publishing, radio and television, script writing, religious work, or journalism.

There are many exciting and satisfying jobs which are not always in the professions or not necessarily the glamorous, "get-rich quick" type represented by sports heroes, rock and roll groups, television or movie stars. Parents and educators need to help students make realistic choices as they search for successful approaches to job attainment and improving their life's conditions.

Attitudinal skills necessary to the world of work and leisure are important to discuss: getting to work on time, getting along with others, being responsible for assigned job duties, cooperating with supervisors and managers.

An appreciation of the world of work and the development of planning and decision-making skills can be initiated within a prescribed school curriculum. The innovative teacher realizes that attitudes and values that relate to success in the classroom also relate to success on the job. An excellent idea for the innovator beginning a unit on career explorations is to team with the librarian and the guidance counselor in order to assure that the information provided keeps pace with accelerating changes in career education.

Educators must experiment with ways to involve students in decision-making. Activities should also aim at including parents and other individuals in the community in the educational process. Earning a living is a subject relevant to all humans at every stage in life. Parents should participate actively with their children in the special programs that deal with careers.

SETTING THE STAGE FOR CAREER EXPLORATION

Arouse in students the realization that everybody is "something" in life, and that often only through careful planning and preparation is that "something" achieved. The idea is to make students believe very strongly in the fact that one's life should be "programmed" for success, not to chance or expedience.

Talk about the "Let's pretend" games children play when they act out roles as doctors, storekeepers, teachers. Ask students if they played such childhood games. Youngster's interests and hobbies often develop into career directions. Do any of the students have favorite hobbies that might develop into jobs? These are usually non-threatening ice-breakers in getting a dialogue going in the classroom.

Then ask students to take a typical day in their lives and consider the numerous workers they encounter. Talk about the variety of jobs. The "somethings" become the milkmen, grocers, bankers, postmen, bakers, butchers, farmers, television repair people, custodians, teachers, etc. with whom they came in contact.

1. Ask the class to make a list of local business and industrial firms where they might look for a "first job" during their high school years, either after school or during holidays and summer vacations. The list might look like this:

   Barber shops
   Beauty salons
   Automobile service stations
   Automobile repair shops
   Supermarkets
   Dairies
   Restaurants
   Drug stores
   Department stores
   Factories

2. Next, ask students to select from these suggestions several hypothetical places where they might enjoy working.

3. Direct students into clustering job options at these sites into two areas: service jobs, and goods producing jobs.

4. Last, have each student list various sources of information about job choices. (The librarian and the counselor will be resource people at this step.)

Every day students participate in situations where people are working and never think about whether these business or industrial occupations might afford them a job option at some time in their lives. These four steps will help to introduce job awareness.

CAREER EXPLORATION IS MULTIDISCIPLINARY

There are many options for exploring careers within subject classes. By incorporating a career module into his or her curriculum, each teacher can help students to explore career information related to that particular field. New ways of making goods and products, changes in living standards, revisions in psychological and social aspects of work are constantly changing the types of jobs that are available. All these factors necessitate teachers' working closely with students on career developments within their fields of specialization.

Every student participant should learn answers to questions such as these: What kind and how much training and education are required to enter a particular occupation? How do earnings in certain occupations compare with earnings in other occupations requiring similar training? Is my temperament suitable to certain jobs? What technique could be applied to modify my behavior patterns to qualify for better job options? What kinds of equipment are used in certain job clusters? What environmental and working conditions are associated with particular occupations?

Within every subject area there will be opportunities to bring up the subject of earning power. You can start by discussing allowances. In order not to cause students embarrassment, begin with a general question like "How many of you earn your own spending money?" Next, proceed to find out what teens do to earn money and what kinds of things they want to buy. Then develop a discussion on how peoples' wants affect the job market.

You can provide Social Security applications. Some will already have cards but most will consider applying for cards an adult activity—a step in preparation for the world of work. Invite a representative of the local Social Security agency to discuss the benefits of participation in the program. This information service is offered free in every community where there is a Social Security office.

CAREER EXPLORATION ACTIVITIES

1. Introduce the book *Saturday's Child.*[1] Ask each student to seek information from a different chapter and to explain why the biographee selected the job she is performing. Discuss how jobs are stratified according to a status system in a society. How do we determine what is important to us in life? Do we want to play it

---

[1]Suzanne Seed, *Saturday's Child* (Chicago: J. Philip O'Hara, Inc., 1973).

safe in a job choice? Will we take chances? What type of status do we seek from a job?

2. Assemble a series of pictures showing people on different jobs dressed in clothes related to their jobs. Using an opaque projector, you can flash these pictures on a screen and ask students to classify the person on the job as low income level, middle income level, or high income level. Point out discrepancies in the classification by the students.

3. Introduce the "Prologue" to Chaucer's *Canterbury Tales*. Ask students to read aloud descriptions of the different persons who went on a pilgrimage in the fourteenth century. How did society evaluate persons and job titles then? Evaluate, in terms of status, the professions, the crafts, and the religious positions of the fourteenth century. How does modern society's evaluation of the medical profession compare to that time in history? Compare an astrologer's status in our own society with that of an astrologer in the fourteenth century.

4. Build test consciousness by asking a representative from the state employment office or a school counselor to administer a typical placement test to the class. Discuss the inequities of evaluating someone on a test basis only. What ways do we measure clerical, numerical, or scientific skills? Mechanical aptitude? Verbal and spatial reasoning? What parts do past performance and references play in evaluation for job placement? Can a language barrier stifle chances for a job?

5. Take an inventory of students who are interested in school. Discuss the relationship of interest to skill development. How can hobbies and sports strengthen abilities that lead to jobs? (For example, can sculpturing as a hobby be helpful to a future dentist? Can building models be a step towards building or designing cars?) Ask students to list classes where they can explore special interests.

6. Ask students to analyze the financial and business pages of their community newspaper. What new companies and services are highlighted? How do they affect the job market? What factors affect job opportunities?

7. Analyze the want ads for information on job availability. How do we respond to ads asking for resumés and applications? Incorporate the techniques of filling out applications and writing resumés in this activity.

8. Analyze the businesses and companies in the community for varied employment opportunities. What causes jobs to increase? What is the range of salaries within a business or company? Invite community representatives to answer students' questions about entry jobs, chances for promotion, and salaries. How do the salaries differ according to years of service, skills, experience, sex, age?

9. Invite a proprietor of a business (e.g., restauranteur, funeral home owner), and a self-employed person (seamstress, caterer, or carpenter) to discuss the pros and cons of being your own boss.

FOCUSING ON PERSONAL QUALITIES

Working hard is important to job success; however, getting along with people is also a very valuable ability, since many jobs require working closely with others. Sometimes there is an important relationship between attitudes, personality traits, and job choice. There are some things students can do to help them recognize and overcome social barriers in attaining jobs and keeping them.

Opening the Dialogue

Ask students to evaluate themselves in terms of what society expects from an individual performing a particular job. Do they have any visible obstacles and is it worth the effort to change patterns of behavior, dress, speech if it means job success? How can one compensate with one's strong personal characteristics to cover the weaker ones?

The Geist Picture Interest Inventory[2] provides a tool for helping students to define interest areas. Projective uses of the results provide a means for gaining insights into why one rejects certain occupational choices. Since the student is encouraged to select one of thirty-five reasons for each interest choice, personal influences and attitudes toward work can be explored by this means.

After administering the interest inventory, evaluate results and discuss the test as one way to better understand oneself in

---

[2]Harold Geist, *The Geist Picture Inventory: Male and Female* (Los Angeles, California: Western Psychology Services, 1964).

relation to others. Discuss male and female choices on the test. Are there sex stereotypes? Are there real differences?

Physical and personality characteristics often influence employment. As a group or individually, have students analyze occupations in terms of any special characteristics that we associate with the jobs. Ask students to discuss the following jobs in terms of requirements, especially of temperament: radio announcer, firefighter, nurse, farmer, flight attendant, teacher, secretary, seamstress or tailor, construction worker, salesperson, accountant.

Use some of the following questions to liven up the discussion and motivate the students to think realistically about the relationships of people who get along together.

1. Name one teacher you admire. What kind of personality does this person reveal? What does this teacher do to keep students interested? What kind of temperament is appealing in teachers? Is there only one type of personality suited to the teaching field? Why or why not?
2. What is the difference between an introvert and an extrovert? How can either of these characteristics be a strength?
3. Analyze four personality traits: initiative, perseverance, reliability, and accuracy. How do these traits relate to success in class; in getting along at home?
4. Ask students to question three to six adults about what three traits they feel are most important in holding a job and getting promotions.
5. Prepare a chart listing traits that help in getting along with other people.
6. Ask students to do some self-evaluating of their relationship to classmates, adults, parents, brothers and sisters. Which personal qualities are *you* lacking? Which can you strengthen?
7. Who are the significant others in your life? In the world of work, how are we dependent on others? How does getting a job done relate to working with others?
8. Invite individuals representing the building trades, crafts, and professions to discuss the vital skills used in getting along with others and the obstacles faced by those who fail to get along with other workers.

Job success doesn't just happen. Some of us think we'll find a lucky four leaf clover and everything will turn out all right.

Sometimes we read our horoscopes for clues to our future. The clues lie within ourselves.

ANALYZING CAREERS AND LIFE STYLES

Here students will be learning the art of reading skillfully while searching through career-centered materials in fact and fiction. Many students develop interests through reading fiction. Their interests can then be transferred to biographical works and other nonfiction sources. This approach to guidance and to an understanding of self in relation to the world of work is especially good in an English class.

Fiction and nonfiction focused on vocations can be used as a unit or all during the year at any level from grades seven through twelve. The unit can facilitate the work of a teacher who wants to guide the potential dropout who is "hot for certainty." The teacher is challenged to stimulate the anxious student and arouse the one who is lying on his back and bring both to a state which involves finding out the how and why. Curiosity will lead students to get background material on occupations. They may find, enjoy, and see the significance of vicarious experiences and feel the relief of questions answered in print.

One of the main purposes of this unit is to give reluctant readers books in which they will become so thoroughly absorbed that it becomes fun to read as swiftly as possible to see what happens next. The writing does not have to be great as long as it gives them the satisfaction of involving themselves in material that seems to represent some of their own ideas and feelings.

The plots and love themes in romantic fiction are particularly attractive to young adult readers. Frequently information about kinds of work, qualifications, advantages, and disadvantages, promotional steps, and working conditions of particular careers become apparent through the conversations and experiences of the main characters. This type of fiction often stimulates the reader to search for additional information in a more factual type of publication.

There are disadvantages in using fiction, however. While fiction usually is more readable than nonfiction, the heroes and heroines in fiction are often unrealistically successful. This tends to mislead students in their expectations, unless teachers make a point of helping students to set reasonable objective for themselves.

Establishing a Dialogue

Biographical reading is an excellent tool for allowing students to grasp real life as portrayed in books. How others overcame barriers to achieve personal goals is brought out naturally through the story. Biography can also be an excellent tool for integrating other disciplines. For example, stress the inter-relationship of history and biography. Ask questions like these to open the dialogue:

1. What is biography? What is the difference between autobiography, collective biography and individual biography?
2. Define history.
3. What (to you) constitutes the basic difference between history and biography?.
4. Is history a study of human personalities woven into events, or vice versa?
5. Does the study of biography ever take on historical perspectives?
6. Are there any similarities between biography and history?
7. Could you locate, in the library, titles of an individual biography in which an era in history is pictured or an historical event described? (Example: Margaret Truman's biography of her father, *Harry S. Truman.*[3])

At some point in the curriculum the majority of teachers will be giving assignment for readings in individual biography. It is here that the innovative teacher will realize the strategic moment for integrating such assignments with career exploration. Taking advantage of any library assignment, the teacher may activate the class to pursue further information relative to their own career choices.

Let us assume that the student has already begun the "factual" study of his career. Now, through this class unit, he can get a triangular picture. On a three columnar sheet prepared in advance by the teacher, students can name three books—one containing

---

[3]Margaret Truman, *Harry S. Truman* (New York: Morrow, 1973).

factual data, one biography and one fiction selection—all dealing
with a career choice that he or she favors.

The innovative teacher can distribute a bibliography to the
class as a "beginning sheet," to which he or she may request that
the class add titles from time to time. As usual, the materials for
teaching this unit should be carefully selected, including not only
heroes and heroines with whom secondary school students will
quickly identify, but also choices which will widen their interests
and lead them to reading nonfiction for enjoyment. For students
whose attention span is short, it is a good idea to introduce career-
oriented collective biographies first, encouraging them to read on
a one-chapter basis. Then allow them to graduate to the longer,
individual biographies.

EVALUATING SUCCESS STORIES

The primary emphasis in this unit will be that of reading
autobiographies. People are important. Many success stories
reveal the dominant influences in the biographee's life. Frequently, these influences began to be felt in high school. That books and
reading played one of the most valuable parts in helping them
achieve success is usually evident by reviewing life stories. The
revelation that the biographee might have undergone some
hardships because of his inability to read and communicate well
(*e.g.,* Malcolm X or Frederick Douglass) is a fact that language
arts teachers, especially, may use as a starting point in opening the
dialogue with reluctant readers.

Autobiographies often provide an important link to more
serious studies of occupations. This inspiration is good, but the
fields are limited because the emphasis is mostly on professionals,
athletes, and superstars. These give a distorted view, as they present a picture of people who have achieved unusual success in
their chosen work. By reading and sharing varied
autobiographies, however, students receive information about
many fields of work.

It is surprising how the collection of biographies has expanded in many libraries to include contemporaries as well as old
stand-bys like Helen Keller and Babe Ruth. Especially good as an
introduction are the ethnic concerns series of "Open Door"

pocket books which are short and written on the fourth grade level. These books are easily read and understood but are not elementary in interest level. That is why they appeal to poor readers as well as other students. Some of the ethnic groups include Indian, Puerto Rican, Black, Mexican, and Anglo-American.

The series, which highlights occupations as varied as restaurant manager, insurance salesman, librarian, and air traffic controller, can be adapted by innovative teachers to many subject areas. Not only are the stories interesting, but each book contains statistical information about job opportunities and job outlook at the end of the autobiography.

So Many Detours, one of the "Open Door" books, is typical of the true personal stories that center on the career choices that people made because of their experience and by chance. None of the stories is about famous people.

"Well, look what's become of our class-ditcher!" Social worker, commercial sales engineer for Peoples Gas, graduate of Kentucky Fried Chicken University, gourmet chef at Hugh Hefner's Playboy mansion, Mallary Jones made many detours before finally taking the weighted gamble of owning a McDonald's restaurant in St. Louis.

Beyond his vocational interest he had personal experiences which played a part in his decision, such as delaying his college education to care for his sick mother, divorcing his wife because she felt they were no longer compatible although he still loved her, being promised a job after a year's training and then not getting it. Even when personal hardships and disappointments seemed behind him, new and troublesome detours were ahead. The realism of his life story and his ultimate success in his career and his family life provide an appealing story.

The last few pages of each of the "Open Door" books center on career guidance. This book is on the food service industry and the information stressed is the nature of the work, the chances for employment, the earnings, working conditions, training and qualifications, employment outlook, and where to go or write for more information.

Another in this series is *Mission Possible.* This book is action packed with thought provoking experiences. Reading the table of contents is a zinger: Teacher Was a Black Belt, In Over My Head, Blaming My Big Chance, Everything Against Us, I'm Going to Kill You. That feeling of defeat in these titles is what Zenolia Leak was ominously surrounded by in her young life. How her life (which seemed to be a Mission Impossible) lead to *Mission Possible* is set out in a fast-paced story.

She shares the demoralizing events in her life that almost shattered her. Then she builds to her present good life and the job where she works "not just for money . . . once you've gone that route you know you have to like what you're doing or it won't work out no matter how much you're paid."

"In high school I got rid of two things I hated: my tag name 'Skinny' and my stepfather." She is about to talk to a group of students who are a lot like she was at that time.

Opening the Dialogue

The teacher can introduce the "Open Door" books by sharing the highlights of one of the stories and perhaps even reading a few passages. The first time around the books can be passed out randomly. Then the students can trade them to read about someone who favored a career field that interest them. The books are a handy pocketbook size, illustrated with photographs and peppered with frank conversations.

We would advise gaining approval to use the books since, on occasion, although not in most of these books, the personal stories include language that may be offensive, and experiences of drug taking, rape and other violence.

An excellent example for the English teacher to use in arousing his or her students to equate success with their mastery of reading skills can be found in the autobiography of Malcolm X.[4] The social studies teacher may use Malcolm X's life story in a study of ghetto life in America.

The teacher could open the dialogue by selecting seven students at random in the class and asking them to read passages from the autobiography. Ask the students to try to empathize with Malcolm as they read:

Student 1: "I became increasingly frustrated at not being able to express what I wanted to convey in letters that I wrote, especially

---

[4]Malcolm X. *The Autobiography of Malcolm X*. With assistance of Alex Haley. (New York: Grove, 1965), pp. 172-174.

those to Mr. Elijah Muhammad. In the street, I had been the most articulate hustler out there—I had commanded attention when I said something. But now, trying to write simple English, I not only wasn't articulate, I wasn't even functional. How would I sound writing in slang, the way I would *say* it, something such as, 'Look, daddy, let me pull your coat about a cat, Elijah Muhammad—!'"

Student 2: "Many who today hear me somewhere in person, or on television or those who read something I've said, will think I went to school far beyond the eighth grade. This impression is due entirely to my prison studies.

"It had really begun back in the Charlestown Prison, when Bimbi first made me feel envy of his stock of knowledge. Bimbi had always taken charge of any conversation he was in, and I had tried to emulate him. But every book I picked up had few sentences which didn't contain anywhere from one to nearly all of the words that might as well have been in Chinese. When I just skipped those words, of course, I really ended up with little idea of what the book said. So I had come to the Norfolk Prison Colony still going through only book-reading motions. Pretty soon, I would have quit even these motions, unless I had received the motivation that I did."

Student 3: "I saw that the best thing I could do was to get hold of a dictionary— to study, to learn some words. I was lucky enough to reason also that I should try to improve my penmanship. It was sad. I couldn't even write in a straight line. It was both ideas together that moved me to request a dictionary along with some tablets and pencils from the Norfolk Prison Colony school."

Student 4: "I spent two days just riffling uncertainly through the dictionary's pages. I'd never realized so many words existed! I didn't know which words I needed to learn. Finally, just to start some kind of action, I began copying."

Student 5: "In my slow, painstaking, ragged handwriting, I copied into my tablet everything printed on that first page, down to the punctuation marks. Over and over, aloud, to myself, I read my own handwriting."

Student 6: " . . . With every succeeding page, I also learned of people and places and events from history. Actually the dictionary is like a miniature encyclopedia . . . That was the way I started copying what eventually became the entire dictionary. It went a lot faster after so much practice helped me to pick up handwriting speed. Between what I wrote in my tablet, and writing letters, during the rest of my time in prison I would guess I wrote a million words."

Student 7: "I suppose it was inevitable that as my word-base broadened, I could for the first time pick up a book and read and now begin to understand what the book was saying. Anyone who has read a great deal can imagine the new world that opened. Let me tell you something: from then until I left that prison, in every free moment I had, if I was not reading in the library, I was reading on my bunk. You couldn't have gotten me out of books with a wedge. Between Mr. Muhammad's teachings, my correspondence, my visitors—usually Ella and Reginald—and my reading of books, months passed without my even thinking about being imprisoned. In fact, up to then, I never had been so truly free in my life."

To demonstrate further the impact of what Malcolm X was writing in these passages, the innovative teacher can walk over to another student and place in his hand an abridged dictionary. Ask the student to quickly turn to any page in the volume. Then instruct him or her to read all of the words given in one column. Encourage students to react to this technique of building vocabulary and learning to read. Pepper the discussion with questions like these:

1. Could you compare your reading habits with Malcolm X's?
2. Have you ever felt inadequate in trying to express yourself?
3. Do you think this inadequacy might be reflected in attempts to to get a job?
4. If you are not inclined to study whole pages of the dictionary or an encyclopedia, do you think there is much to be gained from studying success stories?

Suggested Autobiographies

Anderson, Marian. *My Lord, What a Morning.* New York: Viking, 1956.

Angelou, Maya. *I Know Why the Caged Bird Sings.* New York: Random House, 1969.

Bailey, Pearl. *The Raw Pearl.* New York: Harcourt Brace Jovanovich, 1968.

Boswell, James. *The Life of Samuel Johnson.* (Modern Library Series.)

Brown, Claude. *Manchild in the Promised Land.* New York: Macmillan, 1965.

Buck, Pearl S. *My Several Worlds: A Personal Record.* New York: John Day, 1954.

Chisholm, Shirley. *Unbought and Unbossed.* Boston: Houghton-Mifflin, 1970.

Davis, Sammy Jr. with Jane and Burt Boyar. *Yes I Can.* New York: Farrar Straus & Giroux, 1965.

Devlin, Bernadette. *The Price of My Soul.* New York: Knopf, 1970.

Dooley, Thomas A. *Dr. Tom Dooley: My Story.* rev. ed. New York: Farrar Straus & Giroux, 1962.

Douglass, Frederick. *Life and Times of Frederick Douglass.* (Available in several editions.)

Dunham, Katherine. *Island Possessed.* Garden City, N.Y.: Doubleday, 1969.

Eisenhower, Dwight D., *At Ease: Stories I Tell to Friends.* Garden City, N.Y.: Doubleday, 1967.

Frank, Anne. *Anne Frank: The Diary of a Young Girl.* Garden City, N.Y. Doubleday, 1952.

Franklin, Benjamin. *Autobiography.* (Available in several editions.)

Frazier, Walt. *Clyde,* with Joe Jares. New York: Holt, Rinehart and Winston, 1970.

Gibson, Bob. *From Ghetto to Glory: The Story of Bob Gibson.* Englewood Cliffs, N.J.: Prentice-Hall, 1968.

Golden, Harry. *The Right Time; an Autobiography.* New York: Putnam, 1969.

Hayes, Helen. *On Reflection: an Autobiography,* with Sandford Dody. New York: Evans, 1968.

Jones, Mallory. *So Many Detours,* with R.E. Simon, Jr. Chicago: Children's Press, 1970.

Keller, Helen. *The Story of My Life.* Garden City, N.Y.: Doubleday, 1954.

King, Coretta. *My Life with Martin Luther King, Jr.* New York: Harcourt Brace Jovanovich, 1969.

Leak, Zenobia. *Mission Possible,* with George Elrich and Emmett Smith. Chicago: Children's Press, 1970.

Lenski, Lois. *Journey Into Childhood: the Autobiography of Lois Lenski.* Philadelphia: Lippincott, 1972.

Lopez, Arthur. *El Rancho de Muchachos,* with Kenneth G. Richards. Chicago: Children's Press, 1970.

Malcolm X. *The Autobiography of Malcolm X,* with Alex T. Haley. New York: Grove, 1966.

Mantle, Mickey. *The Education of a Baseball Player.* New York: Simon and Schuster, 1967.

Mikita, Stan. *I Play to Win.* New York: William Morrow, 1969.

Namath, Joe. *I Can't Wait Until Tomorrow . . . 'Cause I Get Better Looking Every Day.* New York: Random House, 1969.

Parks, Gordon. *The Learning Tree.* New York: Harper & Row, 1963.

Robinson, John. *I Never Thought I Had It Made; As Told to Alfred Duckett.* New York: Putnam, 1972.

Sanger, Margaret. *Margaret Sanger: Pioneer of Birth Control.* New York: Crowell, 1969.

Sayers, Gale. *I Am Third.* New York: Viking, 1970.

Schweitzer, Albert. *Out of My Life and Thought.* New York: Holt, 1949.

Steffens, Lincoln. *Autobiography.* New York: Harcourt Brace Jovanovich, 1968.

Vasquez, Joe C., with R. Conrad Stein. *My Tribe.* Chicago: Children's Press, 1970.

Washington, Booker T. *Up From Slavery.* Garden City, N.Y.: Doubleday, 1933.

Williams, Ted. *My Turn at the Bat: the Story of My Life,* with John Underwood. New York: Simon and Schuster, 1969.

Wong, Jade Snow. *Fifth Chinese Daughter.* New York: Harper & Row, 1950.

Wright, Richard. *Black Boy.* New York: Harper & Row, 1969.

A CAREER CASE STUDY

Start the discussion by challenging students to consider a case study of someone currently in the news. For example, encourage them to analyze and compare this life story of an "unknown" with a successful, well-known person. A unit may be constructed around the case study which will permit the teacher to integrate several techniques into the assignment (*e.g.* researching information, speaking, writing, interviewing, role playing and compiling bibliographies.)

An example might be as follows: Diana Ross, a successful singer, compared with Betty Jackson, an unknown. Once the personality is selected, divide students into five groups:

Group 1: Research biographical information on one successful and an unsuccessful singer (In this example, Diana Ross and Betty Jackson).

Group 2: Report on the art of interviewing as an instrument for applying for work.

Group 3: Dramatize the main points of Diana Ross' life by utilizing the techniques of interviewing. Allow two students to engage in role playing.

Group 4: Give instructions on how to compile a bibliography. Demonstrate by listing in correct bibliographical form as many books as you can locate in the library featuring the life of Diana Ross. Have the bibliography mimeographed and distribute copies to the class.

Group 5: Explain the basic points of compiling a bibliography of magazines. Compile a bibliography of magazines in which one could find the stories about Diana Ross' life. (Consult the *Reader's Guide to Periodical Literature.* Listings will include *Ebony*, old issues of *Life, Young Miss, Time.*)

Ask each group to pull materials together in order to share the information and the techniques with the rest of the class.

CASE STUDY A[5]
(Unsuccessful Vocalist)

As a child in Suffolk, Virginia, Betty Jackson had dreams of being a singer or a nurse, and someday a wife. Instead, at 15 she had an illegitimate child and that, coupled with the death of her mother, was the "end of my hopes." Migrating to New York City in 1960, she worked for four years as a live-in maid until another pregnancy caused her to lose her job. She has been on welfare ever since.

Presently living in a four-room ghetto apartment in the Bronx with four of her seven illegitimate children, Betty Jackson says, "I live in dope city and on one of the worst streets. The apartment has been robbed three times, and I've been cut once. We have no heat. We get hot water once in a while. The wall is coming apart from the leaks. I've had a broken window for the past year. The kids sleep in their clothes. I use the stove and oven for heat, but the gas and electricity bills are very high. I had an electric heater once, but it was stolen. Roaches are everywhere. The rats minuet and waltz around the floor."

While welfare pays her monthly rent of $92.10, she says that the additional $128.00 she receives twice a month barely

---

[5]Excerpted from "A Gallery of American Women," *Time* XCIX (March 20, 1972), p. 28c.

allows for the necessities, much less such luxuries as a telephone, radio, T.V. or vacuum cleaner. "I am a slave to my financial problems," she says, "and my life is meaningless as far as having things that people are supposed to have."

Now 36, she says of the three men who sired her children that "I have never come close to getting married." She says that whatever hopes she had of returning to work were dashed when her 19 year old daughter gave birth to an illegitimate child two weeks ago. Survival, she explains, is her primary concern.

Discussion Questions:

1. Does the life of Betty seem to echo a "sense of hopelessness"?
2. Was her life programmed for failure? Do we write our own life script?
3. Do you think Betty merely held empty dreams in her desire to be a singer or nurse?
4. Was there any indication of plans for choosing a career, then working to achieve her goal, either as a child, or now?
5. Were you to give her neighborly assistance, to what agencies in your community would you direct Betty?
6. What books would you refer her to?

CASE STUDY B[6]
(Successful Vocalist)

Diana Ross, the second eldest of six children, was born in Detroit, Michigan on March 26, 1944 to Fred Ross, a factory worker, and Ernesting (Earle) Ross . . . Miss Ross's parents, now separated, still live in Detroit.

When Diana was growing up, the Rosses lived in a third-floor walk-up apartment in the Brewster-Douglass Homes, a low-income housing project in a poor section of Detroit. 'We . . . six kids . . . slept in the same room, three in a bed, with a kerosene lamp lighted to keep the chintzes (bedbugs) away,' she has recalled . . .

Singing in the choir at the Olivet Baptist Church in Detroit was a Ross Family tradition . . . The closest she came to formal voice training was the instruction of the choir director and some coaching in pop singing from an older cousin.
. . .

---

[6]Reprinted by permission from the April 1973 issue of *Current Biography.* Copyright © 1973, The H.W. Wilson Company, pp. 29-32.

After school she worked as a bus girl in the basement cafeteria of Hudson's, a Detroit department store and harmonized on street corners and at social gatherings with two girl friends, Mary Wilson and Florence Ballard. As semi-professionals, calling themselves the Primettes, they made about fifteen dollars a week. Ironically, Miss Ross was rejected when she tried for a part in a high school musical. "You have a nice voice," the teacher in charge told her, "but it's nothing special." Diana, who believes in working hard to achieve her goals, was undaunted by the rebuff.

Meanwhile, in 1959, Berry Gordy Jr., a former automobile assembly-line worker, was launching the Motown . . . Record Corporation . . .

Even before she graduated from high school, Diana Ross was importuning Gordy to hire the Primettes, and to that end she even took a job in his office. As a secretarial assistant she lasted only two weeks, but in the early 1960's Gordy began using the Primettes for background singing in recordings by Mary Wells, Marvin Gaye, the Shirelles, and other early Motown stars, and soon he began grooming them for a career of their own. He renamed them the Supremes.

. . . Miss Ross made her movie debut in the title role of *Lady Sings the Blues* (produced by Berry Gordy and released by Paramount in October 1972) . . .

Discussion Questions:

1. Does the life of Diana Ross seem to exemplify a desire to excel?
2. Was Diana'a life programmed for success?
3. Were there obstacles or hurdles for Diana Ross to overcome in order to succeed?
4. Were there any indications early in life of Diana Ross' plans to be a singer?
5. List five or more references giving additional information on Diana Ross' life.
6. Between books and magazines, which would be the logical choice for the most current information on her life? Why?

HOW WE SEE OTHERS — HOW OTHERS SEE US

Human relations often spell the difference between a satisfying and successful career and one that is boring and unproductive. The following unit also focuses on understanding qualities for meeting job requirements and for overcoming obstacles in attaining a job by examining the successes achieved by others.

Current Biography, a monthly biographical magazine of personalities in the news provides excellent, quick reading material about people who have been recognized for some special achievement. Since how others evaluate us is often the clue to whether we are hired for a job or not, the importance of the job interview is also highlighted here.

An excellent reference tool for allowing students to discover how others have accomplished success in their jobs despite obstacles and hardships, *Current Biography* can reveal a variety of facts for classroom adaptation. For example, the story of Martina Arroyo (är-rō-yō) appeared in the February, 1971 of *Current Biography:*

> . . . young Harlem-bred singer . . . acclaimed in the concert halls and opera houses of the music capitals of Europe. . . Born about 1936 in New York City, Martina Arroyo is the second child of Demetrio Arroyo, who had moved to the United States mainland from Puerto Rico at the age of eleven, and of Lucille (Washington) Arroyo, originally of Charleston, South Carolina. (p. 3)

The story of her struggles and sacrifices appears on pages 11-14 of the 1971 cummulative annual. The same annual offered the facts of George C. Scott's life:

> The grandson of a coal miner and the son of a mine surveyor, George C. Scott was born in the mountain hamlet of Wise, Virginia, in rural Appalachia, on October 18, 1927. (p. 385)

George C. Scott is the talented actor and director.

The April 1973 issue of *Current Biography* carried a fascinating biographical account of Harland Sanders, better known as Colonel Sanders, "The creator, ex-owner, and living symbol of the Kentucky Fried Chicken Corporation." This account tells the incredible Horatio Alger, rags-to-riches story of how a sixty-six year old man amassed a fortune after a lifetime of varied and usually poorly paid jobs.

This brief article is typical of the *Current Biography* write-ups concerning personalities who are prominent in the news. Here is one of the many passages that can offer inspiration to students:

> As the oldest of three children, he inherited family responsibility at the age of six, when his father died and his

mother was obliged to take a job peeling tomatoes by day and sewing by night. Sometimes left alone for days at a time, the children learned to forage for food, and Harland began the culinary education that was to prove so important later. According to a profile of Colonel Sanders by William Whitworth in the *New Yorker* (February 14, 1970), Harland at the age of seven "was excelling in bread and vegetables and coming along nicely in meat."[7]

Since *Current Biography* includes so much information about contemporary personalities, both national and international, it lends itself quite appropriately to use as a reference tool in the study of careers. Articles in it are brief, objective, accurate, and well-documented. A portrait of the biographee usually accompanies the article. Publications of the biographee are usually listed. Information about each biographee includes vital statistics about birth, address, and occupation.

This publication is issued monthly, then bound as a yearbook at the end of the year. Indexes in the monthly issues of *Current Biography* accumulate from month to month until the year's end. Periodically, the bound yearbooks have decennial indexes to previous yearbooks which are so marked on the spine of the yearbook. Each issue of *Current Biography* carries classified lists of persons by their specific fields. This is helpful in gathering names of persons prominent in a given occupation.

Other Handy Reference Tools

The Readers' Guide to Periodical Literature is an index to over one hundred general magazines most often read and enjoyed in school libraries. *Who's Who in America* outlines the careers of notable people living in the United States. *Webster's Biographical Dictionary, The Abridged Dictionary of American Biography,* and *Twentieth Century Authors* are three sources of brief, biographical accounts of well-known persons.

Encyclopedias should not be overlooked as a source of biographical information. For example, a science instructor might plan productive activities for future scientists by assigning names like Galileo or Thomas Edison for library research. Both Galileo and Edison are examples of young men who "dropped out" of

---

[7]Reprinted by permission from the April 1973 issue of *Current Biography,* Copyright © 1973, The H.W. Wilson Company.

school, overcame many obstacles and attained success despite tribulations and disappointments.

OVERCOMING SNAGS IN JOB INTERVIEWS

The job interview is frequently the crucial step that determines whether a person will be hired or not. A teacher can provide a service to students by initiating lively in-class activities that simulate the interview experience. Stressing listening skills and being prepared to answer questions about qualifications, education and experience will provide the student with practical information about the face-to-face experience of the interview. If the student gets practice during class time, he or she is building job entry skills.

Techniques for building interview skills are varied. One idea is to invite the personnel manager of an employment service or local business to visit the class and to interview several students for hypothetical jobs. Encourage the community person to give insightful information about the interview procedure and common mistakes that job applicants make. Several days before the guest arrives encourage teens to compete for the hypothetical job for which they will be interviewed by doing homework related to the job. What does the business or industry produce? What services does it perform? What age person will they hire? What skills are needed for entry? What about advancement?

Ask students to do homework on the place where they think they might seek employment some day. Since the employer is likely to ask personal questions about strengths and experiences and education, students can be taught to answer in a straightforward manner with confidence based on preparation. Sometimes students will be asked about the pay they wish to receive. If they are not sure how to answer, encourage students to raise questions like, "What is the pay scale within the company?" Stress the art of answering and asking questions tactfully.

Students will begin to realize that certain questions are a part of almost every interview. Interest in building interview skills can be heightened by asking students to write a script with an interview format and to use hand puppets to focus on the art of interviewing and the snags the interviewee can stumble on. Project the idea of the part personality plays in the interview and the special importance of coming prepared to answer questions with confidence.

Another valuable technique is that of role playing. Role playing can provide a better grasp of the stress placed on individuals when they are interviewed for jobs. Since talk shows are fun to watch, another successful strategy for building interviewing skills is to have students simulate a talk show interview.

STRUCTURE A JOB STUDY

The teacher should structure a unit and establish work routines in such a way that group or individual projects do not become chaotic. Start the class with preliminary directives, give the dates for completion of assignments, and set up specifics on the use of library and audio-visual facilities. Give general directions on the safe use of necessary tools, designating the proper work areas and cleaning up procedures. Tips on how to properly distribute materials, when to turn to a schoolmate for help, and what to do with remaining time after completion of a project are also important.

A general sample of how to research information on a chosen job cluster follows. You may direct students to be more specific by listing titles of materials, appropriate television or radio programs, and names and addresses of people or agencies to contact:

1. In the school
   a. Materials Center
      Books, pamphlets, magazines
      Films, filmstrips, records
      Slides, tapes, kits
      Career files
   b. Guidance offices
   c. Classrooms
2. In the community
   a. Persons in the various job fields
   b. Public libraries
   c. Vocational-technical schools
   d. Summer jobs; after-school employment
   e. Tours and travel experiences
   f. Employment agencies

3. Other sources
   a. Radio and television classes and programs; movies
   b. Newspapers, magazines
   c. Closed circuit television
   d. Home study courses
   e. Government documents on the local, state, and federal level

Once the dialogue has been established and the interest continues, the teacher may want to use the film "Making It In The World of Work."[8]

Job Study Activities

1. Ask students to enumerate their own "Program to Success," by starting on the bottom rung of the ladder and proceeding to the tenth step by some logical pattern which they have set for themselves (see illustrations on pp. 94-95). Suggest that they indicate the period of time they should use for each step. Start with education.

Ten Steps to Success in Law or Government

Steps	Years	Career Options
10 Seek public office	2	
9 Enter private practice	2	
8 Work for legal defense	2	
7 Earn law degree	3	
6 Work summers	2	
5 Enroll in law school	1	
4 Work 1 year	1	
3 Complete college	4	
2 Finish high school	6	salesperson, clerk
1 Finish elementary school	6	janitor, handyman, babysitter

Let students fill in what job options will be available if they drop out at the different steps. What skills are added and what benefits are earned can also be indicated as they continue to step up.

---

[8]*Making It In The World of Work.* Studio City, California: Filmfair, 1972.

Ten Steps to Success
in a Craft

Steps	Years	Career Options
10 Enter private electrical business		
9 Secure "small business" loan		
8 Receive journeyman's card	5	
7 Secure electrical apprenticeship	4	
6 Enroll in Industrial Training Program	1	
5 Work 1 year in industry	1	
4 Finish high school	2	
3 Get vocational training in senior high school	2	
2 Finish junior high school	2	
1 Finish elementary school	6	

Let students fill in what job options will be available if they drop out at the different steps. What skills are added and what benefits are earned can also be indicated as they continue to step up.

2. Ask the class to study the "Help Wanted" section of the classified ads in the local newspaper. Let students report on what information can be gleaned from these ads about the kinds of job openings, what specifications about age, sex and experience are needed, whether a telephone call or personal appearance is requested, etc. If a letter is required, explain what information will be valuable to an employer evaluating applications. Techniques for writing a letter of application and gaining references for supportive information are vital to the job seeker.

3. Plan a field trip to a U.S. Employment Office, an area industry, a factory, store, or other on-the-job situation. Observe workers, types of work being conducted, the tools and equipment with which workers operate, the job classification of workers, working conditions, hours of employment, salary scale if available, etc.

4. Ask students to check through various magazines, (e.g. *Time, Ebony, People)* and to be on the lookout for descriptions of persons in unusual occupations to discuss and share with the class.

5. Encourage students to write a business letter requesting free documents from their state government and from the U.S.

Government Printing Office, Washington, D.C. 20242. There are all kinds of interesting materials on jobs and work requirements available from these agencies.

6. To encourage systematic gathering of information, ask the class to make personal scrapbooks during this segment of the career unit. In this way materials from different classes would be kept in one place and the student could begin building a perspective about himself in relation to the world of work.

7. Have students compile lists of books available in the library on the careers of their choice. Let the bibliography include both fact and fiction books, and suggest that they be made in the form of bookmarks.

WHAT MAKES YOU CLICK?

For this unit teachers of any subject will be capitalizing on student interests in photography and sound reproduction. While expanding their artistic judgments and continuing their development in creative expression, a new avenue of experimentation may be opened both to innovative teachers and to students through creative taping and photographing on color slide film.

The overall purpose of the unit is to instruct students in the art of photography, in adding sound to their color slides and in producing homemade filmstrips while they are focusing on careers. The students are active participants in learning. They are actually doing the work, and are developing responsibility for their own learning through their interest and participation.

Setting the Stage

The innovative teacher realizes that potential dropouts may be kept zipping through assignments with enthusiasm by borrowing from elementary school teachers the practice of changing both the subject content and physical environment of the classroom from time to time. For example, it is a good idea to rearrange the furniture periodically. The new placement of furniture can usher in a whole new feeling among students. It can heighten their interests in discovering "What's up for today? Everything looks different!"

Let students know that something very different is about to take place by first re-structuring the classroom. Set up booths or stations to accommodate the equipment that will be used. Call the unit something like "Library-Media Workshop on Careers"—to give the students the feeling that everyone must "work" in this "shop," and that all class members are participants.

Establishing a Dialogue

A teacher can begin the discussion by explaining briefly how pictures relate to our everyday life and to the personal enjoyment that we experience through reading books, viewing movies or television stories:

Teacher: Did it ever occur to you that life is a series of pictures un-folding before your eyes? To demonstrate this point, try to remember an incident you might have experienced as a child. Is your memory of this incident a series of pictures?

If you were to stand in front of the class and relate a story you had read, or a favorite movie or television episode, undoubtedly your recollection of these would come as a series of pictures.

Some professional storytellers say that this is an ideal way to remember stories. First, read the passage slowly, let-ting the characters, events and plot of the story develop in your mind. Then close your eyes, letting the pictorial images unfold in your memory. Read the story once more for language and style. Using this technique, it is surprising how much the mind can retain and relate of what has been read.

In a previous unit we enumerated many places of business in our community. Some of them were probably places in which you would like to work. Today, we shall em-bark on a new, a very different activity. Instead of remembering pictures, now we shall photograph them.

Since this is such a different activity, let's give it a dif-ferent name. Let's call it our "Library Media Workshop on Careers." But let's not take ordinary photographic prints for our workshop. Let's take colored slide films. Then let's write a script for each photograph, and let's dub in music to make our production lively!

You can decide now on some potential titles for the production. Here are some examples:

Learning the Job Clusters in Our City
On-the-Job Scenes of Workers in_____
Company
Professional Workers in our Town

People in Service Jobs
People in Goods-Producing Jobs
Views of People in My Chosen Career
Architectural Styles in the City of _____.

After the students have listed their titles, ask them to select classmates with whom they wish to work. Some school budgets make allowances for expenses such as cameras, films, tape recorders and kits for producing slide film. If not, a teacher may find that some students can provide their own cameras and film for this study and that others will bring borrowed equipment.

A typical four-week unit could be planned as follows:

A LIBRARY MEDIA WORKSHOP ON CAREERS

I. Objectives of the Unit.
   A. To teach students investigative techniques for gaining occupational information from the school and community.
   B. To correlate their new knowledge about careers with information about themselves.

II. Goals for Student Performance.
   A. To teach students skills in operating equipment relevant to the workshop (*e.g.,* camera, tape recorder, slidefilm projector, filmstrip projector and record player).
   B. To provide for creative expression through script writing, filmstrip drawing, and taping (*e.g.,* set aside weekly laboratory sessions for this purpose).
   C. To provide instruction in library skills, so that all students will be competent in the following:
      1. Use of the card catalog.
      2. Locating general material (e.g., Career File).
      3. Checking out library materials.
      4. Investigating and tracking down facts; researching information on a specific career.
   D. To provide youngsters with opportunities for discovering other sources of information, both print and non-print, by encouraging them to seek direct contact with community businesses and personnel in various job fields.
   E. To correlate students' experiences during field trips with information obtainable through books and other media.
   F. To hold an evaluation and sharing session, during which *you,* as teacher, parent, or administrator, will listen to what *students* say.

III. Preparations for the Unit.
   A. List all materials students will need to participate in the workshop:
      1. Camera
      2. Color slide film (1 roll).
      3. Flashcubes (2 packages).
      4. Spiral tablet, pen and pencils.
      5. Phono-disc for background music.
      6. A case for storing and carrying all materials and supplies.
   B. Check out library materials needed for the classroom collection.
   C. Order a do-it-yourself filmstrip kit for students desirous of making filmstrips. One type is the "U" Film Kit, available from Hudson Photographic Industries, Inc., Irvington-on-Hudson, New York 10533.This kit provides standard 35mm filmstrip material, along with explanations for use.
   D. Reserve all audio-visual materials needed from the school audio-visual specialist, and make arrangements for storing the equipment overnight until the workshop is ended.
   E. Reserve a room in the library in which students can make tapes.
   F. Have forms typed and ready for distribution before the project begins:
      1. Permission slips requesting parents' signatures if students have to leave the school campus.
      2. Clearance forms from places of business in the community allowing students to snap photos of workers on the job.
      3. Approval from the principal for students to leave the school premises when necessary.
IV. Teaching Students How to Use The Media Effectively.
   A. Ask a photographer to give a simple explanation of how a camera works.
   B. Ask the school audio-visual specialist to explain techniques for effective sound reproduction.
   C. Invite consultants to talk with the class on techniques for the use of camera and tape recorder.
V. Other Guidelines for the Teacher to Follow.
   A. Explain script writing. Offer samples such as the one on page 100.

92424

B. Plan a sequence for photographing slide film and select a phono-disc to dub in while taping the script on a chosen career.

SCRIPT: "A Career in Librarianship"

Frame No.	Slide Picture	Script
1	A CAREER IN LIBRARIANSHIP	A career in librarianship. (Music: "Outa-Space", by Billy Preston. Keep under).
2	By John Doe	By John Doe (Musical curtain).
3	Picture: Exterior of Public Library Building	Here is a picture of the public library I work as a library page three times a week here. I enjoy my work so much that I think I'd like to become a children's librarian.
4	Picture: Inside Children's Room (Circulation Desk)	The children's room is a very beautifully decorated room. I assist here at the circulation desk by checking books in and out of the library.
5	Picture: Storytelling Corner	A favorite nook in the children's room is the storytelling corner. When all of the stools are filled up, we throw soft rugs down for more children to join us in "Storytelling Hour."
6	Picture: Listening Corner	Frequently, I am called on to help a young child operate the listening equipment. A favorite record now is Donny Osmond's.
7	Picture: Children's Libraran	The children's librarian is my boss. She is a warm and friendly person who supervises the staff and all of the functions of the children's room. She has special training to be a librarian for children.

INTERNSHIP: ON-THE-JOB VOLUNTEERS

Come to grips with the concept of bringing the student and his career interests more realistically together. Projects for the classroom become more meaningful when they have vocational content, since the turned-off student is a pragmatic learner.

The concept of a university without walls, used successfully in many institutions of higher learning, can be adapted for senior high schoolers, especially reluctant learners. Teachers may borrow some practices from the Minnesota Metropolitan State College program where "the idea is to provide off-campus independent study and internship programs . . . for students who have become disaffected by traditional education or who are unable to benefit from it."[9]

> Most of MMSC faculty work full time in business, industry, or government; some have never attended college and hold no degrees. Teachers are not recruited for their academic backgrounds, but rather for their proficiency in a particular craft or profession. Likewise, students receive no grades . . .[10]

The mandate is apparent: Allow each student to freely explore what he feels has a clear, demonstrable bearing on what will be relevant to his future career.

Encourage a spirit of volunteerism among students. Check with business firms, industries, and other places of business to see if they would allow students to serve as interns or volunteers while undergoing a series of learning experiences. Plan a community relations program so that students, parents, and the community will understand the idea of training sites away from school. Very important to the success of the program is the scheduling of hours at the job sites and the careful selection of firms to participate.

Students are placed in this internship program in much the same way that medical interns are at teaching hospitals. By participating in a Volunteer Work Corps, students receive on-the-job training while exploring possible careers. As in the Minnesota program, the students can write their own contracts. Parents, community businessmen and women will be drawn into active participation by cooperative contracts. (See page 103 for a sample contract.)

As the teacher encompasses the entire community with projects from his or her classroom, each student will be following an independent course of study carved to his or her own needs as an intern. Thus, the potential lawyer will be observing the mechanics

---

[9]Michael W. Fedo, "A Metropolis as College Campus," *American Education* (April, 1973), p. 8.
[10]Ibid

of law in a lawyer's office and in the courtroom, the aspiring insurance writer will be making the rounds with an insurance salesman, future nurses will be volunteering their services as aides in hospitals and clinics, and the future secretaries will be working in offices. A flexible 6 to 12 week internship program may be set between educators and working establishments comprising the career clusters. Some students may be released earlier from their internship if they have demonstrated competencies within their choice field or job.

Not only school classes but also community activities offer a variety of opportunities for developing interests. On a bulletin board for activities and special events, post notices of art workshops, clubs, community theatre, concerts and the meeting time of civic, political and hobby groups. Encourage teens to become aware of ways others make their lives more interesting and meaningful.

The opportunity to talk with people who are directly involved affords a down-to-earth approach to career information.

CONTRACT FOR PARTICIPATION IN THE
VOLUNTEER WORK CORPS

Name_____ Grade_____ Room No._____

Address_____

      (street number)   (city)   (state)   (zip)

Telephone_____ Parents/Guardians:_____

Address of Parents/Guardians_____ Business phones:_____

Occupations of Parents/Guardians_____

                  (mother)   (father)

My present school schedule:

Period	Subject	Teacher
1		
2		
3		
4		
5		
6		
7		

My Career Cluster:_____

I would like to work as a_____on a volunteer basis for a period of _____weeks, commencing on_____(date) and ending on_____(date) in the following place of business:

_____   _____

Name of working establishment   Manager

_____

Street Address   City   State   Zip

_____

Telephone

The following is a list of the learning activities and educational resources to which I would like to be exposed during my internship as a member of the Volunteer Work Corps:

_____

_____

_____

_____

This contract has the approval of my parents/guardians and the manager whose names are affixed below:

Signature:_____ Company_____

       mother

Signature:_____ Signature:_____

       father

                          Title: _____

                          (Manager, President, etc.)

5

Teaching Critical Thinking

Thinking that we can answer all of our personal questions by turning to the horoscope daily guide can be humorous—and sometimes tragic. If students have difficulty coping with frustrating school problems, it is very unlikely that they can find the answers in a horoscope guide. However, teachers can capitalize on students' interest in horoscopes to motivate them to achieve academic success.

Sometimes we are struck by prejudicial lightning and resist change in our manner of presenting assignments to our students. We need not accept student control of subject matter to be taught, since that could mean the abdication of our educational responsibility; however, we can add vitality and sharpness of purpose to our present teaching strategies. Since most people seem to find time to do the myriad of things they enjoy and in which they are interested, let's motivate teens by capitalizing on subjects they really enjoy.

For example, the following experiment was made to coincide with a teacher's assignment for reluctant readers:

A school librarian carefully selected several books about astrology, signs of the zodiac and mysteries of the mind. She then procured a cart from a neighboring supermarket and dumped the volumes in this cart to overflowing capacity. The cart was decorated with bright, multi-colored streamers before it was pushed out into the main reading room at an angle which required most of the library's patrons to either go around it or stop in front of it. As expected, most of the students stopped to examine the cart, and some ended up checking out several of the books. Many of the students visibly changed from dull, reluctant patrons to highly motivated and eager readers.

The point dramatized by the experiment was not so much that students read what was set out for them conveniently, or what was displayed attractively—although both were contributory factors—as it was that students literally gulped down what interested them and enticed their imagination. What the school librarian and teacher learned was that the occult sciences make stimulating and intriguing topics for teens.

The teacher's task is to correlate intriguing topics with educational objectives. These activities can be centered on improving communication skills through assignments involving the analysis of propaganda and thought control in the communications media; creative writing and effective speech; and reading for enjoyment. Teachers of social studies and language arts can build units incorporating many high-interest activities as focal points for class motivation.

DREAMS AND FANTASIES

An escapade, a journey, a scene, new faces—what an extraordinary dimension of our mind reveals itself through secret, real-life visions in dreams! One moment the dreams are with us, and then they slip away. Day-dreaming and night-dreaming provide us with insights about ourselves and the dimensions of our conscious and subconscious minds. Why not begin this segment of the topic by allowing students to escape into a dream world? Such an exploration can get this unit off to a vigorous start with students unearthing and examining data on the world of dreams. Dreams embrace a dimension of experience and memory different and apart from our normal world and our natural sphere of living. Let's examine dreams in many literary forms and styles.

Using the *Secret Life of Walter Mitty*[1] as a reference point, students can read how Mitty escapes into a dream world where he

---

[1] Harold P. Simonson, ed., *Trio: A Book of Stories, Plays, and Poems,* 3rd ed. (New York: Harper & Row, 1970).

can fantasize his wildest wishes. After reading this short story aloud, encourage students to imitate this man be comparing fantasy answers and actual responses that might have occurred in situations like these:

Fantasy Response   Response

> a. During an argument
> b. When you were with someone you really liked
> c. When a teacher asked you to recite in class
> d. When a parent criticized you
> e. When you were afraid of something

Building Discussion

Students often like to share stories out of their dreams. This is another way to keep discussions moving in the classroom. The English teacher can allude to dream-like experiences of characters from different forms of literature.

Jacob's Dream: The Old Testament

There are many incidents of dreams recorded in the *Bible*. As an example the teacher can quote this description of Jacob's dream of the ladder reaching up to heaven:

> And he dreamed, and behold a ladder set up on the earth and the top of it reached to heaven: and behold the angels of God ascending and descending on it.
> And, behold, the Lord stood above it, and said, I am the Lord God of Abraham thy father, and the God of Isaac: the land whereon thou liest, to thee will I give it, and to thy seed;
> And thy seed shall be as the dust of the earth, and thou shalt spread abroad to the west, and to the east, and to the north, and to the south: and in thee and in thy seed shall all the families of the earth be blessed.
> And Jacob awaked out of his sleep, and he said, Surely the Lord is in this place; and I knew it not.
> (*Genesis*, Chapter 28, verses 12, 13, 14 and 16)

Related Activities

1. Analyze the analogies and discuss their significance in this passage.

2. Rewrite the passage into modern English.
3. Draw a poster depicting the scene.
4. Discuss what precipitated the dream.

Scarlett's Nightmare in Gone With the Wind[2]

A good example of how the dream of the main character in a novel is repeated in the plot is dramatized in Margaret Mitchell's historical classic about the South at the time of the Civil War, *Gone With the Wind*.

One student gave this account of Scarlett's description to Rhett of her recurring "nightmare":

> Scarlett begins by confiding to Rhett that at times she attempted to be nice to people and kind to Frank. But then she would have the frightening nightmare again, and the impulse to go out and grab money, whether it was hers or not, would return.
>
> Rhett soothes Scarlett and encourages her to describe the nightmare in detail. In her description, Scarlett reveals her first reactions to Tara, her home, after her mother's death, when the Yankees had burned down everything. She is hungry, always so hungry in the dream. So are Pa, the girls, and the slaves who keep expecting her to help them.
>
> Scarlett describes her escape in the dream, where she is running into a gray mist. She explains her feeling that she is being chased, that she feels she must reach her destination; only then would she be safe. After waking from her dream, it always seems to Scarlett that she has never lost her hunger nor her fear. Frank, by his slow manner, made her lose her temper with him. Even though she promised herself she would make it up to him someday when she was no longer hungry, when they had enough money to allay her fears, that day never came before his death. Scarlett regrets, too late, the wrongness of it all.

Discussion Questions

1. Why would someone have a recurring dream? Are they troubled?
2. Do you resolve problems in dreams?
3. State a personal conflict. Then fantasize in a dream-like sequence in written form how the conflict was distorted and finally resolved within the dream.

---

[2]Margaret Mitchell, *Gone With the Wind* (New York: Macmillan, 1936). See page 828.

Additional Activities

1. Contrast family life portrayed in parts of the book with family life as we know it today.
2. Describe how economic conditions in the South differ in the twentieth century from what it was like in the nineteenth century. (Research the information to support your point of view.)
3. Predict what you think family life will be like in the year 2000 A.D.
4. Predict what you think the economic condition of the U.S. will be like in the year 2000 A.D.
5. Arrange to see the movie version of *Gone With the Wind* as a class activity.
6. Draw a poster depicting your image of Scarlett "running into the gray mist."

Lady Macbeth's Sleep-Walking Scene

The teacher can use a play to provide the student with an enjoyment of drama, while at the same time introducing her or him to Shakespeare's poetry, his masterful use of imagery to exact mood and idea, and his skillful choice of words. Many Shakespearean dramas are unsurpassed in their classical beauty.

Lady Macbeth's sleep-walking scene, in the short play *Macbeth*, can be read and students can discuss the visible effects of anxiety on a person's mind and body. In Act V, Lady Macbeth, driven by fear and guilt after the murder of Banquo, walks in her sleep and tries to wash away the blood stains that she imagines are still on her hands. Her doctor admits he can do nothing for her "infected mind" and suggests that she needs divine forgiveness more than she needs a physician.

Shakespeare, William. *Macbeth* (many editions)
Act Five
Scene I
Dunsinane. Anteroom in the castle
(Enter a Doctor of Physic and a Waiting Gentlewoman)
Doc. I have two nights watch'd with you, but can perceive no truth in your report. When was it she last walk'd?
Gen. Since his majesty went into the field, I have seen her rise from her bed, throw her nightgown upon her, unlock her closet, take forth paper, fold it, write upon it, read it, afterwards seal

it, and again return to bed; yet all this while in a most fast sleep.

Doc. A great perturbation in nature, to receive at once the benefit of sleep, and do the effects of watching. In this slumbery agitation, besides her walking, and other actual perform- ances, what (at any time) have you heard her say?

Gen. That, sir, which I will not report after her.

Doc. You may to me, and 'tis most meet you should.

Gen. Neither to you, nor any one, having no witness to confirm my speech.
    (Enter Lady Macbeth, with a taper)
Lo you, here she comes! This is her very guise, and, upon my life, fast asleep. Observe her, stand close.

Doc. How came she by that light?

Gen. Why, it stood by her: she has light by her continually, 'tis her command.

Doc. You see her eyes are open.

Gen. Ay, but her sense is shut.

Doc. What is it she does now? Look how she rubs her hands.

Gen. It is an accustom'd action with her, to seem thus washing her hands; I have known her continue in this a quarter of an hour.

L.M. Yet here's a spot.

Doc. Hark! she speaks, I will set down what comes from her, to satisfy my remembrance the more strongly.

L.M. Out damned spot! out I say! One: two: why then 'tis time to do 't: hell is murky. Fie, my lord, fie, a soldier, and afeard? What need we fear who knows it, when none can call our power to account? Yet who would have thought the old man to have had so much blood in him?

Doc. Do you mark that?

L.M. The thane of Fife, had a wife; where is she now? What, will these hands ne'er be clean? No more o' that, my lord, no more o' that; you mar all with this starting.

Doc. Go to, go to; you have known what you should not.

Gen. She has spoke what she should not, I am sure of that: heaven knows what she has known.

L.M. Here's the smell of the blood still: all the perfumes of Arabia will not sweeten this little hand. Oh, oh, oh!

Doc. What a sigh is there! The heart is sorely charg'd.

Gen. I would not have such a heart in my bosom for the dignity of the whole body.

Doc. Well, well, well, —
Gen. Pray God it be, sir.
Doc. This disease is beyond my practice: yet I have known those
     which have walk'd in their sleep, who have died holily in
     their beds.
L.M. Wash your hands, put on your nightgown, look not so pale: I
     tell you yet again Banquo's buried; he cannot come out on's
     grave.
Doc. Even so?
L.M. To bed, to bed; there's knocking at the gate: come, come,
     come, come, give me your hand: what's done, cannot be un-
     done: to bed, to bed, to bed.

                                                                  (Exit)

Doc. Will she go now to bed?
Gen. Directly.
Doc. Foul whisperings are abroad: unnatural deeds
     Do breed unnatural troubles; infected minds
     To their deaf pillows will discharge their secrets:
     More needs she the divine than the physician.
     God, God, forgive us all! Look after her,
     Remove from her the means of all annoyance,
     And still keep eyes upon her. So good night:
     My mind she has mated and amazed my sight:
     I think, but dare not speak.
                                     Gen. Good night, good doctor.
                                                              (Exeunt)

Additional Activities

1. Play the full-length record, "Macbeth," for class analysis.
2. Attend a Shakespearean play with the class.
3. Assemble a "Glossary of Shakespearean Terms" as a class project.
4. Dramatize and tape scenes of the play using class members as
   actors.
5. Analyze and explain all segments of the drama which portray
   Macbeth or Lady Macbeth in a dream-like or sleepwalking state
   of mind or body.

Abou Ben Adhem

An image "in the mind's eye" is a frequent occurrence when a
person reads or listens to poetry, or listens to the lyrics of a song.
A teacher can build an awareness of imagery as a resource of vivid

experience. All people have imagination and this can be cultivated.

As a technique to erase monotony and boredom, play student-selected records to provide background music that matches the mood of the poetry to be read. This may sharpen students' analyses of the poem's tone, its sound effects, its rhythmical movement as well as its message.

The following poem is quite appropriate:

Abou Ben Adhem (may his tribe increase!)
Awoke one night from a deep dream of peace,
And saw, within the moonlight in his room,
Making it rich, and like a lily in bloom,
An angel writing in a book of gold:—
Exceeding peace had made Ben Adhem bold,
And to the Presence in the room he said,
"What writest thou?" —The vision raised its head,
And with a look made of all sweet accord,
Answered, "The names of those who love the Lord."
"And is mine one?" said Abou. "Nay, not so,"
Replied the Angel. Abou spoke more low,
But cheerly still; and said, "I pray thee, then,
Write me as one that loves his fellow-men."
The angel wrote, and vanished. The next night
It came again with a great wakening light,
And showed the names whom love of God had blessed,
And lo! Ben Adhem's name led all the rest.[3]

Leigh Hunt

Discussion Questions

1. Are there any allusions, symbols present in the poem?
2. Does the poem express an underlying message? What is the message?
3. From the language of the poetry, what images of time and characterization are "felt" by you, the reader?
4. Close your eyes and imagine yourself in Abou Ben Adhem's place; describe the setting.
5. What adjectives would you use to suggest the mood expressed in this poem?

---

[3] Helen Ferris, *Favorite Poems Old and New;* Selected for Boys and Girls (Garden City, N.Y.: Doubleday and Co., Inc., 1957), pp. 565-566.

The Diary of Anne Frank

The personal diary has long been neglected as an example of a literary form, although it vividly documents and expresses the personality, age, and mood of the writer in such a way that it frequently reads like a novel. The autobiographical content of the diary makes it an extremely useful social and historical document and helps in our understanding of what the writer's life was like at the time the diary was kept, as well as what life was like around him or her.

One well-publicized diary about World War II is *Anne Frank: The Diary of a Young Girl.*[4] The diary is an intimate story of a fourteen-year-old Jewish girl who, with her family, hid from the Nazis in a warehouse in Amsterdam, Holland. She was eventually captured, and later died in a concentration camp.

A Drug-Induced Fantasy: *Go Ask Alice*[5]

A more contemporary diary is *Go Ask Alice* which, because of its startlingly vivid descriptions of the contemporary drug scene, has already been forcefully presented as a television movie. The anonymous fifteen-year-old author reveals a discriminating insight into today's troubled youth culture. The writer describes in excruciating, dream-like detail her last encounter with "acid", before her mysterious death:

> I found out how I got the acid. Dad says that someone put it on the chocolate covered peanuts and I guess that's right because I remember eating the peanuts after I'd washed the baby. At the time I thought Mr. Larsen had left me a surprise. But now that I think about it I don't remember why I thought Mr. Larsen had been there and gone without saying anything. That part is a blank. Actually I'm amazed that I remember anything. But I guess no matter what kind of damage I pile on myself, my mind keeps working. The Doctor says that's normal because it really takes a lot to knock your brains loose permanently. I hope that's right because I feel like I've taken a lot already.
>
> Anyway, I remember that the candy reminded me of Gramps because he was always eating chocolate peanut

[4]Anne Frank, *Anne Frank: The Diary of a Young Girl.* (Garden City, N.Y.: Doubleday & Co., Inc., 1952).

[5]Anonymous Author, *Go Ask Alice* (Englewood Cliffs, N.J.: Prentice-Hall, 1971), pp. 125-26.

clusters. And I remember starting to get dizzy and sick to my stomach. I guess I tried to call Mom to ask her to come over and get me and the baby when I realized that somebody had tripped me. It's all very unclear because when I try to think back it's like I'm looking through fuzzy, colored lights but I do remember trying to dial home and taking eternities to get each number to the end. I think the line was busy and I don't really remember what happened next except that I was screaming and Gramps was there to help me, but his body was dripping with blazing multi-colored worms and maggots which fell on the floor behind him. He tried to pick me up, but only the skeleton remained of his hands and arms. The rest had been picked clean by wriggling, writhing, slithering, busily eating worms which seethed on his every part. They were eating and they wouldn't stop. His two eye sockets were teeming with white, soft-bodied, creeping animals which were burrowing in and out of his flesh and which were phosphorescent and swirled into one another. The worms and parasites started creeping and crawling and running toward the baby's room and I tried to stomp on them and beat them to death with my hands but they multiplied faster than I could kill them. And they began crawling on my own hands and arms and face and body. They were in my nose and my mouth and my throat, choking me, strangling me. Tapeworms, larva, grubs, disintegrating my flesh, crawling on me, consuming me.

Gramps was calling me but I could not leave the baby, nor did I want to go with him for he frightened me and nauseated me. He was so badly eaten I could barely recognize him. He kept pointing to a casket next to his and I tried to get away but thousands of other dead things and people were pushing me inside and forcing the lid down on me. I was screaming and screaming and trying to claw my way out of the casket, but they wouldn't let me go.

From the shape I'm in now I guess when I tried to get the worms off me, hunks of flesh and hair came out in my own hands. How I cracked my head I don't know. Maybe I was trying to beat the bummer out of my skull, I really don't remember it seems like such a long time ago and writing this down has made me incredibly tired. I have never been so tired in my life.

Discussion Questions and Activities

1. What emotions do you experience when reading this passage? pity, fear, etc.
2. Do your images of this passage contain color, movement, feeling?

3. Do you perceive any symbols? allusions?
4. Draw a psychedelic picture of this segment of the diary.
5. Make a collage suggested by passages in the book.
6. What is Alice's relationship to the baby?
7. Invite a representative from a drug enforcement agency to discuss LSD and its effects.

ASTROLOGY

Students are interested in astrological predictions, not only in reading their own horoscopes, but also in learning about how their parents and how boy or girl friends "rate with the stars." Activities to match their natural inquisitiveness in this area can be woven into the social studies and language arts curricula.

Fortune-tellers, clairvoyants, prophets, psychics, mediums, seers—practitioners of mind reading—have been known for ages. Early astrologers foretold wars, plagues, and victories. Modern day predictors are frequent guests on radio programs and also subjects of biographical works. Reading about astrological predictions can be a way of whetting a student's appetite to understand a time in history different from his or her own.

As an introductory assignment, why not tie in the relationship of history to astrology while encouraging a group of students to trace the development of astrology from Babylon, Greece and China to our modern Western world? Students will be learning the principles of researching historical information as well as gathering background information on the birth of an age-old subject.

CHARTING ACTIVITIES FOR ZODIAC ENTHUSIASTS

A teacher can start with the known groups of stars called constellations that seem to resemble animal shapes, and then explain that priest-astrologers marked off the "zone of the sky" containing twelve of the constellations and called this the zodiac circle of animals.

Ancients from the Orient gave animals strengths and characteristics that brought luck or ill fate. Combining intuition and intelligence with insight, many writers have written stories, especially children's stories, about these fortune indicators.

Focusing on this theory, the English teacher or social studies teacher can help students uncover myths and their meanings within different cultures.

In *Magic Animals of Japan*,[6] a children's story book about animals with legendary characteristics, students can observe how fact and fiction are woven into a tale. For example, this storybook indicates that a child in Japan is expected to be born with the same traits as the animal of his birth year. Students may refer to the lunar calendar in *The World Almanac*[7] to learn which of the twelve legendary animal names corresponds to the year of their birth. Then they may make analogies about their own characteristics and those ascribed to the animal. For example, if a person was born in the Year of the Tiger, a prediction might be that he or she would be independent and aggressive.

Myths related to predictors of the future are a rich source for story telling and fun-reading. Ask students to write a short essay about a person who reflects his birth sign in his appearance or his actions. Select one of the "Years" from the Japanese legend. Classmates can determine how a student's personal characteristics compare to his predicted ones.

Some students may choose to write an essay or a short story which involves the use of one's imagination. This was written by an eleven-year-old seventh grader:

ZULA

My friend and I saw a cave and went inside. In the cave Sherry and I saw a lot of colored rocks. Then, out popped little green creatures about three inches high. At first, I thought they were midgets. But then, they didn't look like people. They had hair that was red and eyes that were all white with one little purple dot inside.

"Hello," I said. They both laughed at me and began to chirp to each other. One of them motioned to us to sit down on the colored rocks we had seen when we came in.

He chirped, "Beega on Lopkins, please!" "Hi!" said the ugly one, "I do speak same, Do ya! I am Zulain. He is Zipher.

---

[6]David Pratt and Elsa Kula, *Magic Animals of Japan* (Berkeley, California: Parnassus Press, 1967), p. 26.

[7]For example, The 1974 *World Almanac and Book of Facts* (New York: Newspaper Enterprise Association, 1973), p. 357.

Welcome to town Zula! What you here fo! We been livin' peacea for long time. You come in war?"

"No! We just wanted to see the inside of this cave. We did not know that anything was inside."

"Wellz, noz you've seen, be gone!"

So, nice and peacefully we left. Wow! I'll never forget what a gasping and exciting experience it was. I guess that's why I had to tell it to you. Sorry I left out some details, but you can't write everything you know on a piece of paper.

Lynn Gibson

A teacher can harness students' natural interest in astrology to motivate them to write autobiographies which reflect their future goals and an analysis of special personal qualities. In writing the autobiography, ask students to select one of the famous personalities from the student's month of birth—one whose career matches the student's choice of career. Using the accompanying form, a student can draft an outline comparing his or her life script with that of the famous person's life. Urge students to pay particular attention to the special qualities of the biographee, and to notice how the person overcame adversities or obstacles to attain his or her station in life. Goad them on to research more information on the person's life through the use of biographies and the biographical reference works discussed in Chapter 4.

An Astrological Autobiography

Zodiac Sign___Aquarius___
Career Cluster___Science___
Write a comparison of your life with a famous_____scientist_____;

(Career type)

___Galileo___
(Person's name)

HIS LIFE	MY LIFE

Birth date:
    b. 1564, Pisa, Italy. Father
    was a merchant. Full name
    was Galileo Galilei.
	My Birth data:

Early Childhood:
    In early childhood, Galileo
    showed unusual skill in
	My Early Childhood:

HIS LIFE	MY LIFE
building different toys, talent in playing musical instruments, and was a gifted painter. His father encouraged him to study medicine.	
Education: Studied at the University of Pisa. He had to leave the university because of lack of funds in 1585.	Education/Education Desired:
Special Qualities: High I. Q. Perseverance Multi-talented	My Special Qualities:
Projected Characteristics: (What a Guide Book says about those born under the ___aquarius___ zodiac sign)	My Actual Characteristics:
Obstacles Overcome: Although he had to leave school, he continued to study and to develop his mind. Many people misunderstood his teachings, as they differed from those of Aristotle. His use of the telescope led to conflict with the church over the Copernican theory that the earth moves around the sun. After a long trial, he was sentenced to a prison term. He never went to prison, however, because he recanted his position. He was confined to his villa in Florence where he continued to do research.	Obstacles to Overcome:

HIS LIFE	MY LIFE
His Contributions: Conceived the idea of the laws of the pendulum at age of 20. Discovered the famous law of falling bodies at 25. Invented the sector (draftsman's compass) in 1597. Made practical use of the telescope. Discovered the four bright satellites of Jupiter, 1619.	My Secret Aspirations:

Reference Sheet of Some Famous Personalities
Born Under the Various Zodiac Signs

ARIES (March 21 to April 19)	Marlon Brando, Clare Boothe Luce, Julie Christie, Arturo Toscanini, Vincent Van Gogh, Tennessee Williams, Charlie Chaplin, Thomas Jefferson, Washington Irving.
TAURUS (April 20 to May 20)	Sugar Ray Robinson, Audrey Hepburn, Willie Mays, Barbra Streisand, Daphne de Maurier, Harry Truman, Sigmund Freud, Johannes Brahms, Benjamin Spock, Ulysses S. Grant, Fred Astaire, Bing Crosby, Salvador Dali.
GEMINI (May 21 to June 20)	Ralph Waldo Emerson, Walt Whitman, Frank Lloyd Wright, Cole Porter, Bob Hope, Jean-Paul Sartre, Laurence Olivier, Ian Fleming, Rosalind Russell, John F. Kennedy, Marilyn Monroe, Bob Dylan, Nikki Giovanni.
CANCER (June 21 to July 22)	Rembrandt, John Quincy Adams, Henry David Thoreau, John D. Rockefeller, Calvin Coolidge, Helen Keller, Pearl S. Buck, Oscar Hammerstein II, Ernest Hemingway, Louis Armstrong, Gertrude Lawrence, Nelson Rockefeller, Saul Bellow, Marshall McLuhan, Andrew Wyeth, John Glenn, Ingmar Bergman, Gina Lollobrigida, Ringo Starr.
LEO (July 23 to August 22)	Napoleon, Sir Walter Scott, Alexandre Dumas, George Bernard Shaw, Henry Ford, Herbert Hoover, C.G. Jung, Mae West, Aldous Huxley, Alfred Hitchcock, Dag Hammarskjold, Fidel

	Castro, Jacqueline Kennedy, Princess Margaret, Princess Anne.
VIRGO (August 23 to Sept. 22)	Queen Elizabeth I, Goethe, William Howard Taft, Maurice Chevalier, John Gunther, Greta Garbo, Lyndon B. Johnson, Ingrid Bergman, Leonard Bernstein, Lauren Bacall, Peter Sellers, Sophia Loren.
LIBRA (Sept. 23 to Oct. 23)	Franz Liszt, Eleanor Roosevelt, T.S. Elliot, Dwight D. Eisenhower, William Faulkner, George Gershwin, Helen Hayes, Truman Capote, Mickey Mantle, Brigitte Bardot, Julie Andrews, John Lennon.
SCORPIO (Oct. 24 to Nov. 22)	Martin Luther, Marie Antoinette, Theodore Roosevelt, Marie Curie, Pablo Picasso, Marianne Moore, Jawaharlal Nehru, Charles de Gaulle, Katherine Hepburn, Dylan Thomas, Billy Graham, Richard Burton, Grace Kelly.
SAGITTARIUS (Nov. 23 to Dec. 21)	John Milton, Beethoven, Mark Twain, Winston Churchill, James Thurber, Noel Coward, Margaret Mead, Mary Martin, Frank Sinatra, Maria Callas, Julie Harris, Sammy Davis, Jr.
CAPRICORN (Dec. 22 to Jan. 19)	Joan of Arc, Isaac Newton, Benjamin Franklin, Alexander Hamilton, Edgar Allan Poe, Woodrow Wilson, Albert Schweitzer, Carl Sandburg, Rebecca West, Mao Tse-tung, Humphrey Bogart, Cary Grant, Marlene Dietrich, Richard Nixon, Martin Luther King.
AQUARIUS (Jan. 20 to Feb. 18)	Francis Bacon, Galileo, Mozart, Lord Byron, Franz Schubert, Charles Darwin, Abraham Lincoln, Charles Dickens, Franklin D. Roosevelt, John Barrymore, Babe Ruth, Clark Gable, Tallulah Bankhead, Charles Lindbergh, Leontyne Price, Kim Novak, Mia Farrow.
PISCES (Feb. 19 to March 20)	Michelangelo, Handel, George Washington, Victor Hugo, Chopin, Ellen Terry, Albert Einstein, Enrico Caruso, Rex Harrison, Harry Belafonte, Elizabeth Taylor.

Activities to Culminate This Unit

1. Encourage students to be creative, to have fun during writing exercises. Ask students to escape into a dream world and

write about a dream experience in which they acquired fantastic skills, beautiful physical features, or other assets. Encourage students, especially those who are stymied by assignments that are too esoteric, to complete the following subjunctive statements: If I could have. . .; if I were selected . . .; if I had been born with . . .

2. Ask students to write 3 to 5 sentences appealing to one of the five senses: smelling, hearing, seeing, tasting, touching. Play records of poets who appeal to the senses. What do your senses detect as having special meaning for you? What is the sixth sense (*e.g.*, thirst, hunger, pain, muscular movement) that we hear discussed? What is the seventh sense? Some people call this extrasensory perception. Encourage students to discuss personal experiences when unexplained phenomena occurred that seemed to indicate a seventh sense.

3. Invite a professor of psychiatry from a neighboring university or ask a local psychic to visit the class.

4. Write an essay on the relationship between astronomy and astrology.

5. Schedule a debate between believers and nonbelievers in astrology.

6. Let students chart predictions for themselves and for some class members, prophesying what will happen within the next decade.

7. Have students write out predictions for the future of their hometown. Try to foresee the growth or decline of the city in specific areas like industry and government, agriculture, housing and business development; medical, dental, and other professional services.

8. Seek out a personal problem; examine this problem by yourself; find your own solution to the problem

9. Record in vivid detail a recent dream. What symbols were present? How would you interpret your dream? Why?

10. Conduct "before" and "after" surveys, analyzing student beliefs in the powers of astrology before and after the unit was studied.

Suggested References

Aylesworth, Thomas G. *Astrology and Foretelling the Future.* New York: Franklin Watts, Inc., 1973.

Brill, Dr. A. A., ed. *The Basic Writings of Sigmund Freud.* New York: The Modern Library, 1938. (See Book II: "The Interpretation of Dreams," pp. 181-549).

Hyde, Margaret O., *et al. Mysteries of the Mind.* New York: McGraw-Hill, 1972.

Jennings, Gary. *The Teenager's Realistic Guide to Astrology.* New York: Association Press, 1971.

Lynch, John, ed. *The Coffee Table Book of Astrology.* Rev. ed. New York: The Viking Press, 1967.

Ryder, Beatrice. *Astrology: Your Personal Sun-Sign Guide.* New York: Fleet Press Corp., 1969.

At the completion of the unit on "Signs of the Zodiac," students will have a keener awareness of themselves, of their attributes as well as their shortcomings. Now, lead them into units designed to make their habits work for them, through reading newspapers and magazines and televiewing.

One unit allows students to delineate the effects of television in their everyday lives through newscasts, commercials, and program selections. The objective will be to lead each student from an analysis of self to an analysis of the forces in the world around him through the media of mass communications. Still another unit highlights critical thinking through the technique of analyzing photographs.

READING NEWSPAPERS AND MAGAZINES

"What's hap'ning, man!?" seems to be a common teen salutation. Well, lots of things are happening in the world. People are literally assaulted every day with information disseminated by all kinds of media. It is easy to be knowledgeable about what's happening. However, it is another task to be well-informed. Teens, like adults, may become confused by conflicting presentations in the media. Sometimes, one hardly knows what to believe, or how to think.

How and what teen-agers think is important. The teen-ager, more than anyone else, is in a strategic position to influence change in our society. Radical change cannot come overnight, but with gradual and careful planning, teens' ideas can be the prototype for tomorrow's world. For this reason, it is extremely important that students learn critical analyses and interpretation of information. The teacher should carefully steer students away from mechanical, robot-like submission to propaganda. She or he must teach students to *think* for themselves, to learn how to reason beyond what is in print, and to check more than one source to verify information.

Teachers of social studies and language arts can alert students to the powers of persuasion by teaching them the value of reading or hearing what the "other person" says about an issue and analyzing his unexpressed thoughts. Encourage students to examine as closely as possible the message of the communication, the time and manner in which the message was sent, and then attempt to understand the purpose for its transmission. It has been wisely noted that newspapers are printed not only to report the news but also to sell the paper.

To begin the discussion, encourage students to bring examples to the classroom of fallacious thinking in advertisements from newspapers and magazines. Let them examine some of teens' perennial favorites for hidden bits of propaganda:

American Girl	Karate Illustrated
Black Sports	Motor Trend
Black Stars	The New Ingenue
Boy's Life	Popular Electronics
CO-ED	Popular Mechanics
Ebony	Popular Photography
Field and Stream	Reader's Digest
Glamour	Seventeen
Hairdo	Sports Illustrated
Hot Rod	Teen
Jet	Young Miss

The student can cut out advertisements principally, but she or he should also be aware of magazine covers, articles, cartoons, and news clips which influence attitudes. The representations should be convincing. As students become accomplished at shooting down propaganda, their ego strength expands and they gain confidence in presenting their points of view.

DISSECTING ADVERTISEMENTS—KEY TO PERSUASION

One separate activity involves teens' participation in advertisement dissection. Teens will study the many factors governing an ad's influence on people: age, financial status, sex, wants and needs, experiences, mood. One class activity is to select at least four ads for dissection and pinpoint the propaganda that is used to arouse the potential buyer and to sell the product.

The criteria for evaluating the ads should answer the following questions:

1. What basic emotion is aroused by the ad—fear, love, hope . . .?
2. To what age group is the ad appealing? Indicate what you think the nature of the reading audience is: Young children? Teens? Young adults? Hip? Conservative?
3. Which propaganda technique is being used: (a) Strong emotional appeal attached to a stereotype; (b) Statements that make those who aren't interested in the product look stupid; (c) Selected facts which endorse the positive aspects of the product and ignore its shortcomings; (d) Exaggerations about performance or usefulness; (e) Positive associations with related life in the environment; (f) Appeal to an authority.
4. When did the ad appear? Indicate time of day, season, holiday, other?
5. Besides the verbal message, what other kinds of messages are being sent?

THE VIDIOT BOX

If a television set were capable of talking to children, without a doubt there would be some programs it would caution them against viewing. When parents and other adults allow television or movie going to take on parental substitute or baby-sitting chores, children become vidiots. They are no longer discerning viewers. Children, their minds naturally more impressionable than those of adults, are often caught in the make-believe, whirlwind throes of sex, violence, mini-newscasts and commercials expounding their products as "the best." Yes, the television set *can* talk to children through hidden as well as obvious messages.

It is estimated that the average American devotes at least six hours daily to televiewing. Students need to learn how to discern quality and demonstrate good taste in their judgment of what to view. Encourage teens to be thoughtful program selectors.

TEACHING CRITICAL AND ANALYTICAL TELEVIEWING

Opinions help shape the environment in which we live. The teacher can set the stage for this study by beginning the class period with questions related to television programs of the previous evening:

●What, in your opinion, are some of our most pressing political or social problems?

●Were there references to any of these problems on the television programs you viewed?

●Are the major problems of the world presented on day-to-day television shows or radio programs?

●Is the stress on sensationalism, information, or entertainment?

Ask students to begin analyzing what they are watching. Instead of being mesmerized by the picture on the television set, students should condition themselves to listen and watch for information and intensify their analytical abilities. The intent is to teach students to recognize that just because they view something on television, that does not make it valid or unbiased.

Radio and television talk shows frequently engage individuals in discussion on controversial topics. When possible, the teacher can turn on or assign a television program or a news broadcast for class listening and viewing. Encourage students to point out emotional or illogical positions. Tell them to watch for realistic attitudes on the program that help the viewer form his opinions.

Regular television features can be assigned to be watched as an encouragement for students to become conversant with the world's current issues, to analyze character formation and plot development in stories. Some excellent features on social issues are presented weekly. There are many issues in our fast moving world that require understanding of both sides of a situation. As important as it may be to read the world's great literature, today's news and entertainment are also important.

A questionnaire to provoke discerning analysis and open discussion can be used to culminate this study:

Probing for Answers

1. Do you watch television? Daily? Sometimes? Occasionally? Never?

2. What purposes does it serve for you? Entertainment? Sedative? Protection against boredom or loneliness? Information? Other?

3. What is your favorite television program?

4. What have you learned from viewing this program?
5. Do the newscasts ever influence your thinking? If so, how?
6. Do the commercials ever influence your buying? Your parent's buying? If so, how?
7. Have you ever copied hair styles, clothing, gestures, speech mannerisms from any characters portrayed on television programs?
8. Do you think televiewing can persuade one to change a lifestyle? Ethical standards? Moral codes?
9. What are your thoughts concerning the use of the following on television: Profanity? Violence? Racial, religious or sexual themes? Nudity or semi-nudity? Tobacco, drugs, or alcohol? Explain your position.
10. What set of codes would you, as a televiewer, establish for the following television presentations: Newcasts? Daytime serials? Talk shows? Variety shows? Television specials? Weekly dramas? What else?
11. How do people request what they would like to see on television when it is not scheduled? Experiment: investigate procedures (*e.g.*, write a letter, make a telephonc call, formulate a petition, form a committee to make personal contact with the channel.) Report your results.
12. How do people change what they see and don't like on television? Experiment: investigate procedures (see examples above). Report your results.

Media Projects

1. Make collages of propaganda, using examples of both words and pictorial devices.
2. Research the history of major news agencies in this country. (For example: United Press International, Associated Press.)
3. Write an article for submission to a newspaper or teen magazine.
4. Discuss hobbies, avocations, volunteer work, or other activities that can replace watching television.
5. Compare the news delivered by network radio stations with headlines in newspapers and magazines.
6. Compare the news offered by television networks with news reports in big city newspapers and in national news magazines.
7. Compare lead stories in newspapers with those in periodicals giving weekly news digests.

8. Establish criteria for dissecting a news article.
9. Research the term "yellow journalism." Where did it get its name?
10. Test journalistic reports by hindsight. Go to *Time*, *Newsweek*, or *U.S. News and World Report* magazines of a year to three years ago. Examine issues for predictions and alarms which since have proved false.
    a. Were the errors in judgment excusable in light of the facts available then?
    b. Can the alarm be traced to the prejudices or private aims of those who made them?

PHOTOANALYSIS

Another medium for developing students' critical abilities is through the technique of photoanalysis. This technique—the art of studying and uncovering feelings, expressions and relationships between people pictured in snapshots and other photographs; analyzing how people consciously and unconsciously express attitudes in photographs; and by learning to read body and facial language—was explained in the April, 1974 issue of *Glamour* magazine.[8]

The authors, Dr. Akeret and Mr. Humber, contend that it is possible, from photos, to examine an individual and determine something about his or her personality. After studying the photograph once, "we should go back and scan it to see what we've missed so far. Start with the upper left corner and read the photograph from left to right and downward as you would a book. Take your time; look for unusual details."[9]

After noting the obvious details like dress and facial expressions, the observer should not jump to conclusions but should look in depth, noting every detail before slowly reaching a conclusion. For example, on a family snapshot, items observed like toys, snuggling of smaller children to favorite relatives, body slanting or head tilting toward favorite relatives, are all indications of perceptive photoanalysis.

---

[8]"How to Uncover Hidden Feelings in Photographs," *Glamour*, April, 1974, pp. 172-75. From the book *Photoanalysis* by Dr. Robert Akeret. Ed. by Thomas Humber (New York: Peter H. Wyden, Inc. 1973).

[9]*Ibid.*, p. 174.

When students learn photoanalysis, the technique can be carried over into other areas, such as studying the frames in filmstrips and in moving pictures. Also, students may learn that when looking at cartoons in a series, they can uncover unifying themes. Once the themes are found, then students can get down to really defining the meanings conveyed in pictures.

A SET OF WHEELS

Teachers of English and social studies can also use a topic on "wheels" to teach students critical thinking and to develop in them responsibility for personal property. A unit on "A Set of Wheels" needs no special generator to make it "catch fire" with students, especially boys. Most teens are already preoccupied with learning to drive and owning their own cars. Some teens are already borrowing the family car. However, most students cannot afford cars, but do own bikes. Bikes allow for getting around, breaking the monotony, and providing independence. A set of wheels is one of the teenager's first adult possessions.

BUYER BEWARE

Owning your own wheels means assuming new responsibilities and obligations. Teens frequently think only in terms of the new hot rod or jazzy new car and fail to consider that owning an automobile also means costs of operation, finance charges and installment contracts, insurance coverage and repair bills. An astute teacher can provide his or her students with valuable techniques to help them make value judgments related to car ownership. Comprehending reading material is important preparation for future responsibilities. The reluctant reader can readily see the value of understanding legal documents when they relate to his or her car. The teacher can gather different kinds of contracts, insurance policies, automobile titles, etc. to build awareness of how the written word can be misinterpreted. Each student can review several insurance policies and learn their advantages before he selects one to purchase.

The teacher can write to the various automobile manufacturers in Detroit, Michigan for free brochures, questionnaires and, possibly, movies appropriate for class use.

The driver's manual can be obtained from the local license bureau. Community members such as new and used car dealers and salespersons, insurance salespeople, and Better Business Bureau personnel can be invited to the classroom to give first hand information about the realities and pitfalls of car ownership.

LANDSCAPE DETECTIVES

Protecting oneself and others is a responsibility of automobile and bike operators. Since this same responsibility is important for all who share in the ownership of our good earth, a teaching unit can correlate the responsibility for owning and operating "wheels" with an understanding of ecology.

An intriguing way to teach is to provide students with investigative skills. "Landscape detectives" is an intriguing way to describe students who investigate bike trails, who map out trips, analyze urban planning concerns, discuss the energy crisis and transportation problems, and learn about ecologically valuable places in the community and in the world. Practical skills in reading a map, an atlas, a globe can be built into the lessons, as students map out ways to reach different places.

The social studies teacher can draw students into discussion about the energy crisis and transportation problems. What degree of personal sacrifice will people accept to solve their problems? A comparison between the past and the present ways of traveling can be investigated in terms of changes that have taken place in society.

These early lessons can start with the student drawing a simple, local map and focusing on an urban or rural environment. The teacher can encourage the student to pinpoint notable sites, landforms, and waterways en route. What is the condition of the community that is passed through? What kinds of improvements need to be explored? The students will begin to become trained observers.

EXTEND YOUR NEIGHBORHOOD

Lead students to plan an imaginary visit to another state. Have them write a summary of the characteristics of that state.

Let the summary include the capital city, population, form of government, the places of interest, motto, state bird, flower, major industry or agricultural products, and places of historical significance.

Some students can trace routes to colleges and universities, or major parks within the state. Mileage scales, federal, interstate, local and state highways that will be traveled to reach schools and parks can also be located. In this way, students will learn that they can find their way outside of their own communities with the help of maps and charts. Also, they will gain information about other places.

A MOBILITY MODULE

This mini-module will guide students in the interaction of people and data, and people and land. Travel agents can discuss the tools they use in planning trips for others. By the end of this module, students will have acquired the basic knowledge of how to read a road map, how to determine ways to conserve fuel on trips, how to plan a geographical adventure, and how to assume the basic responsibilities involved in owning one's own "wheels." In this unit, students will also learn about time zones, barriers to communication, characteristics of different areas, and the symbols and requirements of travel.

Motor club headquarters and gasoline companies are places to obtain free road maps for teaching purposes. Information on maps is keyed by numbers, letters and symbols. The social studies teacher can include skill building in cartography within his or her lesson plans. Students will begin to understand problems in transportation, the concept of distance between cities, states and nations, and points of interests outside their living area.

Topographic sheets, nautical and aeronautical charts, atlases, globes, road maps—these tools can be utilized as students become explorers of the world. Navigators such as truck drivers, ship commanders, airplane pilots can be invited to speak to social studies classes about their responsibilities in training for their careers. Emphasis on how each reaches his destination can provide the student with the incentive to begin this unit of study.

Start with the game shown on page 130.

A ROTARY ADVENTURE*

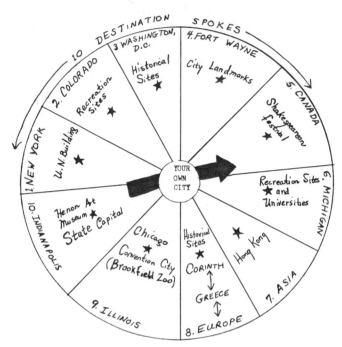

Some destinations are specific; others are general. All are starred ★

DIRECTIONS: Players spin the arrow for choices on the diagram. The variations in possible destination make this game an exciting adventure in which the entire class can engage.

OBJECT: Play the game by researching places of interest, reading road maps and planning a trip.

TO PLAY: 1. Draw a map with instructions on how to get to the destination.
2. Write to Chambers of Commerce or national travel bureaus for places of interest.
3. Write several paragraphs describing the places of interest you will visit.

―――――――――

*Adapted from the game with the same title by the authors of this book.

Additional Auto-Oriented Projects

- Build-it-yourself race car kits can be bought inexpensively and can be used to motivate students to read for directions, information and to complete a project. Young men are usually interested in the results of this type of activity; however, girls frequently like the challenge of putting kits together, too. The social studies teacher can direct a lesson on reading directions. The kits can be started in class and completed at home.

- Crossword puzzles for the non-mechanically minded can include items on style, names of autos, interior design terms, and minor engineering features.

- The teacher can meet with the class in an open area where a car can be brought in—the school parking lot, for example. After a class discussion on how to change a tire, the teacher can point out the differences between doing something and describing how to do it.

- Ask students to write down the systematic preparations necessary for a person to undertake before leaving on a trip. Indicate preparations for oneself, for the car, and for one's home. (*e.g.* have needed immunizations, brakes and tires checked, newspaper discontinued.) Ask students to give supporting reasons for these special arrangements.

- List driving tips for a safe and enjoyable trip. Include summer and winter driving hints, mountain driving, desert driving; what to do in case of bike or car trouble, or an accident; and what to do if a car becomes stranded without gasoline or because of severe weather conditions. Invite a representative from a motor club or from the auto industry to speak to the class about travel and safety hints.

Helpful References You Can Use

Ayer Directory: Newspapers, Magazines, and Trade Publications. Philadelphia: Ayer (published annually).

Cunningham, Chet. *Your Wheels; How to Keep Your Car Running.* New York: G.P. Putman's Sons, 1973

Frankel, Lillian, and Frankel, Godfrey. *Bike-Ways (101 Things To Do With a Bike).* New York: Sterling Publishing Co., Inc., 1972.

Grant, Bruce. *Know Your Car and How to Drive; Hints and Tips to Stay Alive.* Chicago: Rand McNally & Co., 1962. (paperback)

Rand McNally Road Altas. (latest ed.)
Richmond, Doug. *How to Select, Ride and Maintain Your Trail Bike.* Tucson, Arizona: H.P. Books, 1972 (paperback)
Time-Life Editors. *The Time-Life Book of the Family Car.* New York: Time-Life Books, 1973.
Warren, Asa. *North American Bicycle Atlas.* 3rd ed. New York: Crown, 1973. (paperback)
State maps, city maps.
A U. S. atlas.
Miscellaneous maps from motor clubs, local gasoline stations, travel bureaus, etc., according to need.
Also encyclopedias, travel guides, gazeteers, geographical dictionaries and texts.

6

Student-Centered Library Projects

Children seem to change with the onset of summer. The same youngsters who practically had to be dragged out of bed to get ready for school are now up with the summer sun and outside riding bikes and playing baseball.[1]

This phenomenon may seem difficult to understand at first, and there are probably as many reasons for it as there are students. Perhaps the main factor is that school attendance is forced on the student, whereas summer adventures are not.

When children enter kindergarten, they are led to feel that they are embarking on an exciting adventure. The preschooler is often asked by adults how old he is, and upon hearing that the child is near school age, they exclaim, "Oh, then you'll be starting to school this year!" Parents add to the sense of pleasant anticipation by outfitting him with new clothing, pencils, tablets, crayons, scissors, paste, etc.

It appears that many things in the child's early years cause him to eagerly anticipate school. Yet, frequently in a pitifully short period, his attitude changes: school becomes drudgery. The student loses his zest for learning new things.

---

[1]Richard Simms et al., "Making School Fun Again," *Theory Into Practice,* XII (October, 1973), p. 238.

It is the teacher's duty to constantly re-evaluate his or her program, keeping both materials and teaching methods exciting and purposeful.[2] Educators can break the monotony in classroom instruction by zeroing-in on activities for which students motivate themselves because they are *interested.*

INDIVIDUALIZATION

One underlying and recurring theme in student-produced publications, in phono-discs that teens rate high on popularity scales, and in complaint-oriented rap discussions with high schoolers today is that they want to be themselves and to express their own individuality. They insist that they be recognized as separate entities from their schoolmates and their families. Musicians have written about this theme in songs such as "I Gotta Be Me" and "Thank You (for Letting Me be Myself)." Poets like William Ernest Henley have created poems like "Invictus" which, when interpreted broadly, offers the same line of thought. And more recently, under the title *The Me Nobody Knows,* an anthologist culled the poetic voices of ghetto children to reflect their individualistic interests and concerns.

The theme also runs in many autobiographical books, like *I Always Wanted to Be Somebody,* by Althea Gibson, or Sammy Davis Jr.'s *Yes I Can.* Both titles suggest the real importance of expressing and realizing the dreams and aspirations of the "id."

It was Sigmund Freud who differentiated between one's id and his ego: the *id* representing a person's "primitive self," the *ego* one's "ethical self." According to Freud, a child's world primarily reflects the unorganized psychic energies called the id—whose main purpose is the gratification of instinctual needs. As the child grows older, that part of the id which comes in contact with the environment through the senses is modified by the outer world and is inhibited by what Freud calls the ego. This ego, sometimes called the conscience, serves to curb the lawless id, as intrapersonal and interpersonal relations become essential to the child's getting along in society.[3]

---

[2]*Ibid.*

[3]Dr. A. A. Brill, tr. and ed., *The Basic Writings of Sigmund Freud* (New York: The Modern Library, 1938), p. 12.

As more opportunities are provided for students to follow their individuality, they will be better prepared to live productive academic and non-academic lives. The alternative school concept, for example, offers them the chance to exercise more freedom in selecting activities and subjects in which they are interested, rather than following a pre-determined curriculum. Perhaps, the messages of the aforementioned musical and poetic compositions as well as of the complaint-oriented rap sessions are being heeded by progressive educators.

SETTING OBJECTIVES FOR SUCCESSFUL LIBRARY USE

Library research can be the basis for independent and small group study projects. This opportunity for individualization, whether in language arts, social studies or science, increases the importance of the materials center in the instructional system. Printed references embrace a wide range of materials. A few, like general dictionaries and encyclopedias, are frequently introduced to students in their elementary years. Others, like biographical and etymological dictionaries, are taught in the junior high years. The thesaurus, dictionaries of synonyms and antonyms, and dictionaries of slang and of proverbs, may be introduced in the senior high school. Examples of how literary reference works can be introduced are demonstrated in this chapter.

Today's librarian must function effectively as a curriculum practitioner as well as a media specialist. After all, the frequent assertion that the materials center is an integral part—indeed the heart and center of the school's instructional system—is the simple truth. The librarian should not be an isolated administrator presiding over learning materials and library facilities, but should be one who is actively engaged in serving teachers and students in their curriculum needs. She should be a team member in the classroom, in conference rooms, in departmental meetings, and in work on a one-to-one basis with the patrons of the materials center.

The teacher and the librarian can work together to enhance the curriculum. In the past, every child sat in his assigned seat. Every child participated in the day's discussion as best he could.

Every child was required to read the same assignment at the same pace. Every child had to pass the same tests at designated times throughout the year. Then, every child was passed on to the next grade—and there the cycle repeated itself for another grade level. Today our emphasis is on encouraging individual learning modes and pace to insure student success.

If students are going to achieve success in high school subjects, they need to develop an early appreciation and mastery of literary reference tools and library usage. They need to develop the necessary skills for using the library with facility. This is a task which *each* student must undertake *himself.*

In the past, it was not unusual for the librarian to make her annual rounds of the English classes, showing an introductory film on the library's resources, use of the card catalog, indexes, abstracts and other reference books, as well as how to check out a book. Generally, the rules and regulations of the library were explained in detail. Frequently the librarian's visit culminated with a tour of the library. Students would check out library books, then promptly forget all the other services and functions of the library or materials center. The innovative teacher can prevent this deadlock by working closely with the librarian in advance, and by correlating library use with curriculum.

Stimulate in-depth interest and skill in library usage, by correlating library skill-building activities with specific class assignments. Identify specific literary references for language arts or social studies classes noting the unique characteristics of the different kinds of materials to be studied. Enhance student use of these materials by engaging them in creative, analytical and entertaining activities.

HOW THE MATERIALS CENTER CAN SUPPORT STUDENT ACTIVITIES

We sometimes get bogged down with rules and regulations in library usage. Of course, it is obvious that a certain degree of quiet is important if a reading and studying atmosphere is to be maintained. However, this ideal is frequently overstressed, to the discontent of some library patrons. This is especially true in the small school where separate facilities do not exist for small group conferences, listening and previewing rooms or graphics displays. The main reading room becomes a hodge podge of everything, and it is not always easy to control the noise level in the room.

The librarian can set aside a specific area for absolute quiet, another section for group work where quiet talk may be acceptable, another nook for listening and previewing, and a section for quiet games like chess or checkers. Remember, students have to be trained to be respectful library patrons just as they must be taught how to use specific reference tools. However, this should not be done with an over-emphasis on the "don'ts" of library use. The library materials center should be an inviting and pleasant place where students enjoy multi-media experiences.

For a special project which will be beneficial to students and revealing to librarians and teachers, allow students to construct their own film, filmstrip or sound slidefilm production on "The Uses of a Materials Center," using class members as actors. The students can explain in detail assigned texts and specific references in such a project. The setting, of course, would be the school materials center. (For additional information on filmstrip and slidefilm making, refer to Chapter 4).

Introduce the project with a filmstrip such as "Using the Library" produced by Encyclopedia Britannica Films in cooperation with the American Association of School Librarians. The filmstrip is available from Educational Record Sales in New York, Elmhurst, Illinois and Segundo, California.

The following sample script describes several general encyclopedias and some specific reference books which students could use for a social studies filmstrip or slide-film production.

Social Studies Topic: Learning About a Country

Looking for information for a project? What kinds of information are you seeking? Remember, you should select your library materials according to the *type* of materials desired. (For example, if you're looking for maps, you would use an atlas. If you want something about people's customs, a geography or travel book might help. Or, if you're looking for the story of a person's life, read a biography.

Your first step should be in the direction of the card catalog. It tells you whether the library has any books on your topic, and where the books may be found.

Here are some materials which might help you:

Books (Use Latest Editions)

I. Encyclopedias:

Britannica Junior Encyclopedia
Compton's Pictured Encyclopedia
Encyclopedia Americana
Encyclopedia Britannica
Encyclopedia International
Merit Students Encyclopedia
New Book of Knowledge
World Book Encyclopedia

II. Special Reference Books:

Almanacs — *World Almanac* (Garden City, N.Y.: Doubleday). The standard reference almanac for quick information. Index is in the beginning of the book.

Information Please Almanac (New York: Simon & Schuster).Similar to the *World Almanac;* Indexed at the back.

Atlases— *Rand McNally New Cosmopolitan World Atlas* (Chicago: Rand McNally).

Hammond Medallion World Atlas (Maplewood, N.J.: Hammond, Inc.).

Gazeteers— *Webster's Geographical Dictionary* (Meridan, Conn.: G. & C. Merriam Co.). Lists over 40,000 places in every part of the world, marked for pronunciation, location, description and statistics.

Others— *Lands and Peoples,* 7 vol. (New York: Grolier). Includes colored maps and photographs, along with facts, figures and the text on many aspects of the land and peoples.

McGraw-Hill Illustrated World History (New York: McGraw-Hill). Part Two contains a history of nations.

Statesman's Yearbook, 1966-1967. (New York: St. Martin's Press). Provides information for each country about government, area and population, religion, education, production, commerce, communications, etc.

The World and Its People (La Jolla, Calif.: Educational Marketing and Research, Inc.). a 41-volume inclusive work on the major countries of the world, detailing information on the history, fine arts, literature, music, etc. of each.

Magazines

Reader's Guide to Periodical Literature — The *Reader's Guide* will lead you to the latest articles in magazines.

Other Resources

Don't forget—filmstrips, the globe, newspapers, pictures, public libraries, travel bureaus, the vertical file (pamphlets and clippings), your own home library.

The librarian who listens to suggestions from students can get several ideas for making the media center more attractive:

- Why can't we check out reference books? Audio-visual equipment?
- Let's get some more paperbacks kids like to read, instead of all those classics all the time.
- Why don't we put psychedelic posters on the wall or some Japanese kites on the ceiling? Some really "with it" mobiles might liven it up!
- This furniture isn't very inviting; it's always the same—tables and chairs. And I'm shorter than some of my classmates, why aren't there different table and chair sizes in here?

Ten Simple Steps for Preparing a Bibliography

The essential elements of a bibliographical entry are author, title, and the facts of publication, which include place of publication, publisher and date. (Not every entry will include all of these items of information.) The listing should be arranged alphabetically, and divided according to types of material covered (books, films, filmstrips, kits, periodicals, phonodiscs, tapes and transparencies). A reliable style manual to consult for the bibliographical form for print is Kate L. Turabian's *A Manual for Writers of Term Papers, Theses, and Dissertations* (published by the University of Chicago Press).

Ten simple rules follow:

1. List information in this order: author's surname, given name
   or initials (followed by a period), title of work (underlined and
   followed by a period), place of publication (colon, followed by
   two spaces), publisher (followed by a comma), then date (followed by a period).
2. Use a "hanging indention" for listing each entry; *i.e.,* the second and all succeeding lines should begin four (or eight) spaces
   under the first line for each entry.
3. For works by two or three authors, the names of the second
   and third authors are not inverted.
4. For works by three or more authors, after the listing of the first
   author, the words "and others" or the Latin abbreviation *et al.*
   may be used.

Examples

One author:
> Goldenthal, Allan. *The Teenager Employment Guide.* New
> York: Regents Publishing Co., 1969.

Two authors:
> Schill, William J. and Harold E. Nichols. *Career Choice and
> Career Preparation.* Danville, Illinois: Interstate Printers and
> Publishers, Inc., 1970.

Three authors:
> Cribbin, James J., *et al. The Insight Series—It's Your Educa-
> tion; It's Your Personality; It's Your Life; It's Your Future.* rev.
> ed. New York: Harcourt, Brace and World, 1962.

5. For works which bear no individual's name, use as author the
   name of the publishing agency, organization or association,
   committee or company, as given on the title page or the cover-
   title.
6. When no author can be ascertained, enter the citation under
   the title of the work, underlined.
7. Use the first place of publication when more than one is given
   on the title page.
8. If no date is given on the title page, use the copyright date given
   on the back of the title page.
9. Use "[n.d.]" enclosed in brackets when no date can be found in
   the work whatsoever. Accordingly, use "[n.p.]" when no place
   of publication can be ascertained.

10. For revised editions, follow the title page to designate the appropriate edition (rev. ed., 2nd ed., 3rd ed., etc.), and place the statement immediately following the title. The statement is also followed by a period. Only the publication date matching the edition statement is used in the collation.

Example

Carlsen, G. Robert. *Books and the Teen-age Reader.* rev. ed. New York: Harper & Row, 1971.

Listing Periodicals and Non-Print Materials

Examples of bibliographical listings for other media follow:

FILMS: *Making It In the World of Work.* Studio City, California: Filmfair, 1972. color. 26 minutes.

FILMSTRIPS: *Job Hunting: Where to Begin.* Pleasantville, N.Y.: Guidance Associates, 1972. 2 sound filmstrips: Phono-discs or cassettes. (Part 1: 70 frames, 10 minutes. Part 2: 82 frames, 12 minutes).

KITS: *Crisis of the Environment.* New York Times (newspaper), 1970. 5 filmstrips, 5 records, 5 printed texts.

PERIODICALS: Article in a Journal:

Reiss, A.J., Jr. and A.L. Rhodes, "Are Educational Norms and Goals of Conforming, Truant and Delinquent Adolescents Influenced by Group Position in American Society?" *Journal of Negro Education,* XXVIII (Summer, 1959), 252-267.

Article in a Magazine:

Dragonwagon, Crescent. *Selling What You Write.* Seventeen, August, 1974, pp. 144-146.

PHONO DISCS: *The Glory of Negro History.* Folkways, FC 7752. 12", 33½ r.p.m.

Instruments of the Orchestra. R. C. A., album Les-6000. 2 LP stereo records with

Teaching Guide by Charles W. Walton. 12", 33 ⅓ r. p. m.

TAPES: *A Man's Work*: *Career Education.* International Teaching Tapes, 1972. 5 vol. (10 cassettes each volume with guide).

Your Family Name. Madison: State Historical Society of Wisconsin, 1953. 7½ i. p. s.

TRANS-   *History of Afro-Americans.* Vol. I: The African
PARENCIES: Heritage. Scott, 1970. 16 transparencies with guide.

LET'S WRITE "OLD SAYINGS"!

There are conscious and unconscious parts of our minds that respond to everything we do. Consider our reaction when we spill salt and someone says, "That's bad luck." Do we quickly throw a little salt over our left shoulder to ward off evil? A teacher quickens classroom discussion by proceeding from the known to the unknown. Ask students to list sayings and their meanings remembered from their childhood: sayings such as "Step on a crack, break your mother's back;" "Laugh at the table, talk in bed, the devil will get you by the nape of your head," "Don't open an umbrella indoors." Integrate sayings like the ones given here and literary sayings such as Ben Franklin's "Two can keep a secret if one of them is dead," or the Latin proverb, "He who lieth down with dogs waketh up with fleas," into classroom assignments and discussions.

Do these sayings reflect a certain period of life in society, mores, behavior patterns, interests? After a lively discussion, students can write sayings that are hip now. Do they have emotional appeal instead of factual?

TRACKING DOWN QUOTATIONS

Help youngsters learn more about interesting sayings, their sources and their settings. To get them started, introduce students to important literary resources and encourage them to improve their research skills as they track down more information.

Proverb	Reference
"A seventh son is always a lucky or especially gifted person, often gifted with occult powers."	Leach, Maria, ed. *Funk & Wagnall's Standard Dictionary of Folklore Mythology and Legend.* vol. 2: J-Z New York: Funk & Wagnalls Co., 1950, p. 999.
"The sun never sets on the British dominions."	Brewer, E. Cobham, *Brewer's Dictionary of Phrase and Fable.* rev. by John Freeman. New York: Harper & Row, 1963, p. 816.
"There's many a slip twixt the cup and the lip."	————— ,p.32.
"Poverty is no disgrace to a man, but it is confoundedly inconvenient."	Browning, D.C., comp. *Everyman's Dictionary of Quotations and Proverbs.* London: J.M. Dent and Sons, 1959, p. 354.
"A penny saved is a penny gained (or got)." 17th cent.	————— , p. 443.
"Too many cooks spoil the broth."	Burton, Stevenson, comp. *The Macmillan Book of Proverbs, Maxims and Famous Phrases.* New York: Macmillan Co., 1948, pp. 419-20.
"This is to be taken with a grain of salt."	————— , p. 2030.
"Doubt is the beginning, not the end of wisdom."	Bohle, Bruce, comp. *The Home Book of American Quotations.* New York: Dodd, Mead & Co., 1967, p. 124.
"Only a life lived for others is a life worthwhile."	————— , p. 231.

Proverb	Reference
"Every man shall bear his own burden."	Barlett, John. *Familiar Quotations;* a collection of passages, phrases and proverbs traced to their sources in ancient and modern literature. 14th ed. Boston: Little, Brown, 1968. p. 53b.
"As having nothing, and yet possessing all things."	_____, p. 231.
"Geography has made us neighbors. History has made us friends. Economics has made us partners; and necessity has made us allies."	Simpson, James B. *Contemporary Quotations.* New York: Thomas Y. Crowell, 1964, p. 23.

SPORTS, GAMES, AND METRIC MATH

It has been jokingly stated that if all subject disciplines could be taught through sports, there would be many brilliant students filling class seats. Observe your students' reaction to the Babe Ruth record-shattering feat by Hank Aaron April 8, 1974; or Mark Spitz's Olympic performance; to Bobby Fischer's dethronement of the Russian chess wizard, Boris Spassky, in 1973, or the tennis battle between Billie Jean King and Bobby Riggs. It is not unusual to hear an accurate play-by-play account of these happenings from the mouths of students who hardly ever respond to classroom discussions! What better teaching device, then, could the innovative teacher hope for than sports?

Metric measurements are coming to the United States. We see evidence of the changeover from the present decimal system to the metric system more and more frequently. Using a bit of ingenuity while introducing the metric system to mathematics classes, the teacher can lift from the pages of favorites like the *Guinness Sports Record Book*[4] or the *Guinness Book of World Records*[5]

---

[4]Norris and Ross McWhirter. *Guinness Sports Record Book.* Published at frequent intervals by Sterling Publishing Co., Inc. New York.

[5]Taken from the "Guinness Book of World Records" by Norris McWhirter and Ross McWhirter © 1974 by Sterling Publishing Co., Inc., New York.

problems to convert into the metric system. There are a variety of sports-related records, as well as other entries in these books. For example, in the latter volume the following entry is listed under "Mollusks (Mollusca)":

(Squids, octopuses, snails, shellfish, etc.)

> Largest octopus. The largest known octopus is the common Pacific octopus (Octopus apollyon). One specimen trapped in a fisherman's net in Monterey, California, had a radial spread of over 20 feet and scaled 110 lbs. A weight of 125 lbs. has been reported for another individual. In 1874, a radial spread of 32 feet was reported for an octopus (Octopus hongkongensis) speared in Illiuliuk Harbour, Unalaska Island, Alaska, but the body of this animal only measured 12 inches in length and it probably weighed less than 20 lbs.
>
> (page 99)

Convert pounds, inches, and feet into metric measurements from the above entry.

If several entries which appeal to students are selected, then the teacher is not only able to engage students in a perusal of a factual reference, but also to help students learn to convert from the English method to the coming international metric system.

The teacher can select entries crammed with statistics utilizing inches, feet, tons, pounds, seconds, miles, grams, ounces, degrees F and degrees C, etc. for mathematical assignments. Also, the teacher should note the variability of world records from one year to another. For example, in aviation, progress quickly outdates the newest records.

Another activity which allows the teacher to zero-in on the metric system centers around the book, *The All-Star Athletes Cook Book*, by Oscar Fraley and David Huntley (New York: Centaur Press, 1965). The volume features favorite recipes of the athletes, their biographical sketches and portraits. The recipes can be used as the basis for converting measurements into metric figures.

One other book which the teacher with ingenuity can use with interest is C.B. Daish's *Learn Science Through Ball Games* (New York: Sterling Publishing Co., 1972).

For information on the metric system, one valuable address for the teacher to know is that of the Metric Information Office,

National Bureau of Standards, Washington, D.C. 20234, from which you may secure the following:

- *Brief History of Measurement Systems* with a chart of the metric system. (Catalog No. 0303-01073)
- 15 Centimeter Ruler
- Metric Conversion Card

APPROXIMATE CONVERSIONS
TO METRIC MEASURES

Symbol	When You Know	Multiply by	To Find	Symbol
		LENGTH		
in	inches	2.5	centimeters	cm
ft	feet	30	centimeters	cm
yd	yards	0.9	meters	m
mi	miles	1.6	kilometers	km
		AREA		
in^2	square inches	6.5	square centimeters	cm^2
ft^2	square feet	0.09	square meters	m^2
yd^2	square yards	0.8	square meters	m^2
mi^2	square miles	2.6	square kilometers	km^2
	acres	0.4	hectares	ha
		MASS (Weight)		
oz	ounces	28	grams	g
lb	pounds	0.45	kilograms	kg
	short tons (2000lb)	0.9	tonnes	t
		VOLUME		
tsp	teaspoons	5	milliliters	ml
tbsp	tablespoons	15	milliliters	ml
fl oz	fluid ounces	30	milliliters	ml
c	cups	0.24	liters	l
pt	pints	0.47	liters	l
qt	quarts	0.95	liters	l
gal	gallons	3.8	liters	l
ft^3	cubic feet	0.03	cubic meters	m^3
yd^3	cubic yards	0.76	cubic meters	m^3
		TEMPERATURE (exact)		
°F	Fahrenheit temperature	5/9 (after subtracting 32) Celsius temperature		°C

"Approximate Conversions from Metric Measures" is given on the back of this card, which can also be purchased from the Government Printing Office Bookstore (Stock Number 0303-0168. Catalog No. C13.10: 365/2.)

The National Science Teachers Association (1201 Sixteenth Street, N.W., Washington, D.C. 20036) also furnishes a listing of publications which help teachers introduce the generally-used equivalents in the metric system, as well as a useful comparison of a few basic units (*e.g.,* meter/yard, liter/quart, degrees Fahrenheit/degrees Celsius.) Many helpful publications are suggested from this association.

A natural interest in sports and games can be utilized by teachers through reading incentive kits produced by the Bowmar Co. (622 Rodier Drive, Glendale, California 91202).

"Play the Game" by Robert McAdam is an excellent vocabulary builder. It is designed to increase reading skills, especially in the primary grades, but it is also useful for the high-schooler who is reading below his grade level. The kit includes four highly illustrated, easy-to-read books and four accompanying records which narrate the text. The narration is broken at the beginning of each band with lively music.

The kit focuses on minority groups and women, and highlights biographical information about famous personalities in the world of sports (baseball, basketball, hockey, track and field, boxing, football, judo, tennis, ice skating, golf). A useful teacher's guide supplies the following information on each book: reading level, biographical data, interest words and phrases, and questions which can be used to elicit discussion after reading the stories. The questions are designed to encourage readers to reflect on life's values.

Bowmar also produces the "Gold Cup Games" series (*e.g.,* Motorcycle Moto Cross, Horse Trail Ride and Dune Buggy Rally). These games encourage reading, teach students how to follow directions and provide a variety of other benefits and skill building lessons for team cooperation, friendly competition and self-restraint.

UFO'S AND THE SUPERNATURAL: WHAT'S YOUR OPINION?

The librarian who systematically observes the reading selections of teens can capitalize on their natural inquisitiveness to plan additional student-centered library units. Teens enjoy speculating and arguing about the unknown. This is a part of growing up.

This interest in unsolved mysteries offers a vehicle for the teacher to encourage research and debates on issues.

Are we being studied by beings from outer space? What are UFO's? Are there really flying saucers? Were there really witches in Salem Village? Are there witches today? Is there life on other planets? Was there life of a higher intelligence than ours billions of years ago? Is there such a thing as reincarnation? All of these topics stimulate the imagination. Building learning activities and projects around questions like these makes for lively debate and productive discussion.

Initiating Discussion

A good way to start the discussion in this area is through science fiction. Science fiction gives students the opportunity to imagine, if not predict, what kind of world awaits the inhabitants of the future. (Ecological abuses resulting from man's technological masterworks are treated at length in Chapter 8.)

The subject of science fiction can move students into discussions which encourage them to plan beyond the *NOW* of today and the immediacy of tomorrow, by stretching their imagination to perceive the quality of life in the world of the future. Science fiction gives them an opportunity to be creative and to express differences of opinion.

Exposing Fallacies in Arguments

To develop a point of view based on research and analysis instead of emotionalism and persuasion can be a skill that students will find helpful in and out of the schoolroom. Teens do not readily accept criticism of themselves or their pet ideas. Sometimes they do not listen to the constructive part of the criticism, but feel any suggestion as a cutting thrust to their ego. Teachers can help build ego strength within students by encouraging them to expose arguments that reveal fallacious thinking in discussions regarding books, newspapers and magazine articles read, or from radio and television programs relating to mysteries and unexplained events.

Ask students to select a book from these provocative and informative publications:

Suggested Readings

Cohen, Daniel. *Myths of the Space Age; a Skeptic's Inquiry into the Pseudo-scientific World of Today.* (New York: Dodd, Mead, 1967).

Crichton, Michael. *The Andromeda Strain.* (New York: Alfred A. Knopf, 1972).

Harrison, Harry, ed. *The Year 2000.* (Garden City, N.Y.: Doubleday and Co., 1970).

Holzer, Hans. *Gothic Ghosts.* (Indianapolis: Bobbs-Merrill, 1970).

Hynek, J. Allen. *The UFO Experience; a Scientific Inquiry.* (Chicago: Henry Regnery Co., 1972).

Jackson, Shirley. *The Witchcraft of Salem Village.* (New York: Random House, 1956).

Mazzeo, Henry, ed. *Hauntings; Tales of the Supernatural.* (Garden City, N.Y.: Doubleday, 1968).

Soule, Gardner. *The Maybe Monsters.* (New York: G. P. Putnam's Sons, 1963).

Stearne, Jess. *Door to the Future.* (Garden City, N.Y.: Doubleday, 1963).

Sullivan, Walter. *We Are Not Alone: The Search for Intelligent Life on Other Worlds.* rev. ed. (New York: McGraw-Hill, 1966).

Von Daniken, Erich. *Chariots of the Gods? Unsolved Mysteries of the Past.* (New York: Bantam, 1970). pap.

White, Dale. *Is Something Up There? The Story of Flying Saucers.* (Garden City, N.Y.: Doubleday, 1968).

Assign articles on unsolved mysteries listed in the *Reader's Guide to Periodical Literature* to encourage students to study and analyze real or imagined phenomena. Outlining, taking notes based on the information gained from these articles and books will provide them with skill-building practice in reading, help them develop educated opinions about a variety of issues, and form the bases for logical argumentation and debate.

Ask students to divide a sheet of paper in half. On one side, they are to indicate the strong points of the issue they accept. On the other side, the fallacies they reject. Encourage discussion about how arguments can end, such as conceding, winning but still losing, winning, compromising, fighting, alienation, and stalemate. Ask students to use direct quotes from publications as a basis for class discussion of their arguments, and to research supportive evidence from literary references.

IT IS A LAUGHING MATTER—JOKES AND RIDDLES

Most teens and grownups, too, enjoy jokes and riddles. People from all nations enjoy a good laugh. Some of the most eloquent public speakers use humorous quotations and jokes to establish a rapport with their audiences. A good sense of humor is healthy for both students and teachers.

Start the discussion by introducing students to two standard references. Let them use *Roget's Thesaurus of English Words and Phrases,* edited by R. A. Dutch (New York: St. Martin's Press, 1965) and Webster's *New Dictionary of Synonyms* (Springfield, Mass.: G. & C. Merriam Co., 1968) to list synonyms for the word *riddle:*

> puzzle
> connundrum
> enigma
> problem
> mystery

Teach the use of these important references by directing students to the meanings noted from them. These are extremely valuable reference tools in working out crossword puzzles.

"Brainteasers" give teachers the vehicle for exercising the art of deductive reasoning:

> Frank: If one man has two sacks of grain and another has three
>   sacks, which man has the heavier load?
> Hank: The man with three sacks.
> Frank: No, the man with three has nothing but sacks.[6]

Frequently, there are students who clown around in the classroom, because they don't want to do the assigned work and enjoy being the center of attention. Then, there are those who would really like to be comedians or clowns when they grow up. Learning to tell jokes properly and telling them before a live audience in the classroom can build confidence in public speaking. It also provides students with the opportunity to test their style and their ability to extract laughter from fellow classmates.

For the potential comedian in the class, Mark Wachs' *The Funniest Jokes and How to Tell Them* (New York: Hawthorn Books, Inc., 1968) provides helpful hints on how to remember jokes, how to develop your own style in telling them, and how to inject humor into your speech. Another volume which should not be forgotten in this area is the late humorist Bennett Cerf's *Houseful of Laughter* (New York: Random House, 1963) which

---

[6]David Allen Clark. *Jokes, Puns, and Riddles.* (Garden City, N.Y.: Doubleday & Co., Inc. 1968). Reprinted with permission of the publisher.

contains short stories, anecdotes, cartoons, poems, riddles, by James Thurber, John Steinbeck, Mark Twain, Clarence Day and others.

Among the many engaging books with jokes, riddles and funny tales from other lands which can be correlated with language arts and social studies assignments are:

Carl Withers and Sula Benet. *Riddles of Many Lands.* (New York: Abelard-Schuman, 1956).

700 authentic riddles from practically all of the major countries of the world.

Phyllis R. Fenner, comp. *Time to Laugh; Funny Tales from Here and There.* (New York: Alfred A. Knopf, 1942).

A collection of easy-to-read short stories which are designed to induce laughter.

A STUDENT-SPONSORED BOOK FAIR

Some of the most successful book fairs have been those planned and executed by student clubs (library, book, communication, science, social studies clubs, etc.), for which the students themselves prepared posters, wrote publicity releases, decorated the book fair setting, and supervised the buying and selling of exhibit materials. We have seen libraries come alive with stuffed animals, balloons, Japanese kites, mobiles, posters—all these when teens have put their energies to work!

When one does something he puts his heart into, he usually has drive and enthusiasm to complete the project. By participating in club activities students can develop interests that motivate them to become achievers. Clubs help students feel that school is a good place to be. Since clubs are generally varied, numerous and available, they are an ideal vehicle for learning projects and activities.

Library projects and fund-raising are topics frequently and effectively tackled by club members. Since club activities require that members donate their services, a spirit of volunteerism usually prevails. Volunteerism is a great way to harness the energies of students to reach out to others because they understand the loneliness of trying to find friendship and acceptance among their peers.

A good starter for a club project would be a Paperback Book Fair, though generally instituted by the library, when effectively planned and sponsored by a school club, it can engender much more cooperation and enthusiasm from the entire school population.

Paperbacks can be effectively used in social study courses, language arts studies and in science classes. There are often subject-related clubs functioning from these departments within the school. They can be especially useful for involving reluctant readers, since there appears to be something about the size and weight of paperback books which makes them attractive. And the cost of buying and processing them is minimal in comparison with the hardback book collection.

Club members can write to the Children's Book Council, Inc. (175 Fifth Avenue, New York City, 10010), for help in planning a book fair. Be sure to include in your plans: the location, date and time, personnel, publicity, and visiting schedules for students and members of the community.

A few suppliers for book fairs follow:

Academic National Book Fair Programs
The Academic Building
Saw Mill Road
West Haven, Connecticut 06515

Combined Book Exhibit
Scarborough Park, Albany Post Road
Briarcliff Manor, New York 10510

Consulting Media Corp., Inc.
P.O. Box 391-520 E. State St.
Jacksonville, Illinois 62650

Educational Reading Service
Book Fairs Inc.
320 Rt. 12
Mahwah, N.J. 07430

Also, local book companies may supply paperbacks on a contingency sale basis.

Frequently, book fair suppliers will furnish instructions and suggestions for running a successful fair. Sales slips, student order forms, pre-written publicity releases, and prepared posters will be mailed in a kit several days before the books arrive. A more personal touch is added when club members take the time to prepare their own posters and flyers to send to teachers and students, such as those shown on pages 153-154.

WHEN : APRIL 11th and 12th

WHERE : LIBRARY MATERIALS CENTER

Books for Sale

ALL DAY!

Teacher Preview:

THURSDAY, APRIL 8th has been set aside to allow department heads and teachers to preview, examine and recommend all books. You may find some suitable for classroom adoption or book reports

COME IN, TEACHERS!!

ENCOURAGE STUDENTS TO BUY GOOD BOOKS! (Priced from .50 to $3.95)

- Sponsored By -

THE LIBRARY CLUB

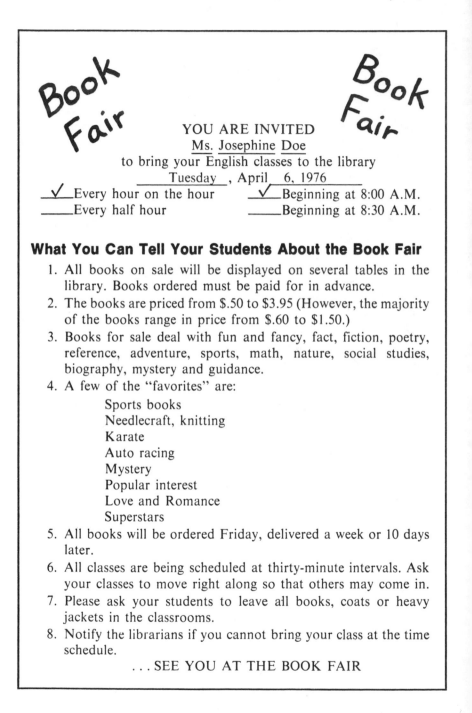

YOU ARE INVITED
<u>Ms. Josephine Doe</u>
to bring your English classes to the library
<u>Tuesday</u> , April   6, 1976

✓ Every hour on the hour   ✓ Beginning at 8:00 A.M.
____ Every half hour   ____ Beginning at 8:30 A.M.

What You Can Tell Your Students About the Book Fair

1. All books on sale will be displayed on several tables in the library. Books ordered must be paid for in advance.
2. The books are priced from $.50 to $3.95 (However, the majority of the books range in price from $.60 to $1.50.)
3. Books for sale deal with fun and fancy, fact, fiction, poetry, reference, adventure, sports, math, nature, social studies, biography, mystery and guidance.
4. A few of the "favorites" are:

   Sports books
   Needlecraft, knitting
   Karate
   Auto racing
   Mystery
   Popular interest
   Love and Romance
   Superstars

5. All books will be ordered Friday, delivered a week or 10 days later.
6. All classes are being scheduled at thirty-minute intervals. Ask your classes to move right along so that others may come in.
7. Please ask your students to leave all books, coats or heavy jackets in the classrooms.
8. Notify the librarians if you cannot bring your class at the time schedule.

... SEE YOU AT THE BOOK FAIR

CULMINATION PROJECTS

- Have students read a mystery play and develop a short story from it.
- Let students write and stage a play from a short mystery story.
- Challenge students to produce a "movie" or sound filmstrip production from a science fiction, mystery story, or other book read.
- Activate the class into writing a report of a ghost story, mystery, or story of strange happenings. Tape the report, dub in appropriate music with eerie sound effects.
- Develop debates on the existence or non-existence of some of the "maybe" monsters discussed in the book by Gardner Soule; unsolved mysteries, such as those in *Chariots of the Gods?* or unexplained scientific phenomena, such as U.F.O's, or life on other planets.
- Clip a supermarket ad from the newspaper. Use sale specials for converting pounds, ounces, gallons, inches, yards, etc. into metric figures.
- Challenge artistic students to draw cartoons providing humorous characters and stories or cartoons providing riddles.
- Draw together a class book of jokes and riddles written by students themselves.
- Assign students to construct test questions in the form of puzzles, jokes, riddles, as the culmination of this unit.

7

Using Varied Media and Resources

Teachers sometimes express frustration at their inability to bring students to a point of concentration, to say nothing of trying to invest them with techniques for critical analysis. How often do teachers say: "Your mind is a million miles away." "An idea goes in one ear and out the other." "Sitting and staring is not concentrating and reading." "Why do I always have to repeat directions?" Yet, there are so many instances of teen's concentrating, exerting determination and tenaciously pursuing "causes" in both study and play that one wonders where the real difficulty lies.

For today's teens, the world offers a never-ending battery of messages in various shapes, forms, and colors exhibited through many communicative devices (not only through drama, music and dance, but also through radio, television, films, books, newspapers, and magazines). All of these media can be used to teach communicative skills, to promote aesthetic appreciation and to enhance cultural vitality in the classroom.

But, it has been said, teaching has not kept pace with technology. Students are forced to live a dual life. The division between what happens in the "outside world" and within the confines of the "school world" is so stark that one may marvel that the schools have any holding power at all. The mass media have made the educational process so sophisticated, some say, that students seem almost to stop learning temporarily in order to attend school.

And once they are in the confines of the school, the printed textbook, the blackboard, pencil and paper—unless careful planning is made to the contrary—dominate the teaching and learning process. Students become controlled by the "monster" bell, which rings at a set time and frequently interrupts students engaged in activities from which they may or may not wish to be interrupted at that particular moment.[1]

Multi-media gadgetry has always been fascinating for students. Even slow-learners like to tinker with mechanical teaching devices. And, too, education is a continuum of experiences: experience plus experience, plus experience *ad infinitum* throughout life. After formal training in the schoolhouse has ended, students continue their learning experiences through activities of their own choosing.

The varied means by which people learn in the real world can be seen as multi-media teaching resources. To the innovative teacher, educational tools and out-of-school activities can offer dynamic approaches for implementing worthwhile learning skills.

GENERAL SUGGESTIONS FOR TEACHING WITH NON-PRINT MEDIA

- Select media on the basis of appropriateness, accuracy and currency of information, age and grade level of students to whom material is addressed, technical quality and adaptability for correlation with printed material being studied.
- Order equipment necessary (*e.g.,* 35mm projector for filmstrips; 16mm projector for moving pictures; overhead projector for transparencies).

---

[1]J. Lloyd Trump and Dorsey Baynham, *Focus on Change; Guide to Better Schools* (Chicago: Rand McNally & Co., 1961), p. 40.

- *Always* check equipment in advance to make certain each item is in working order. (Include extension cords, light bulbs, adaptors, etc. when necessary.)
- Preview materials before presentation; study the teacher's guide, if included; make notes of possible questions to stimulate interest in class; and be prepared to tell the class what to look and listen for in the presentation.
- When necessary, stop the equipment at points in the presentation which may need emphasis or clarification.
- After the presentation, engage class members in a review of the highlights of the material.
- Teach students the operation and care of the various kinds of equipment. Frequently, an audio-visual assistant can be found in each class.
- Where home-made materials are utilized, involve students in their preparation.

MOTIVATIONAL GAMES AND TEACHING TOOLS

One's ability to remember accurately is an important adjunct to learning. Games that strengthen students' memory can form the basis for several worthwhile activities. Teachers of any subject can designate a section of the classroom as a "Game Corner." Here students can become involved in game playing which is either subject-directed and education-oriented, or purely for fun and recreation. For example, the math teacher can allow students to browse freely, individually, or to pair off and play math-related games like TUF. English teachers can involve children in skill-building card games like "Word Power,".

Concentration is a popular card game which requires players to remember the placement of cards on a table. The object of the game is to match cards until all have been removed. Each player turns up one of the cards from the deck placed face down on the table, replacing those for which he has no match. The player holding the greatest number of matched cards is the winner. (It is surprising how adept students become at remembering where the cards are placed, and how experience can enhance concentration!)

Several adaptations of this game are possible. The teacher of remedial English, for example, might use cards listing the various parts of speech (noun, pronoun, adjective, verb, adverb, conjunction, interjection, preposition). A definition or an example of the part of speech can be placed on cards to be matched with the part of speech.

Examples

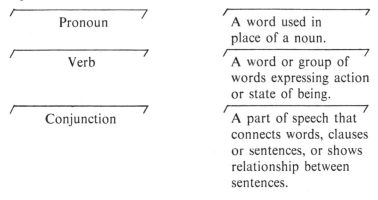

Pronoun	A word used in place of a noun.
Verb	A word or group of words expressing action or state of being.
Conjunction	A part of speech that connects words, clauses or sentences, or shows relationship between sentences.

In a variation of this game, the same cards can be used as "flash cards," to allow students to tutor each other in the game corner. Let one student flash the cards bearing the part of speech before other students who will provide the definitions orally.

Among the many commercial games available are several which we have found particularly effective. Manufactured by the Avalon Hill Company (4517 Harford Road, Baltimore, Maryland 21214), the games are programmed to supplement educational units in mathematics, English, history, geography and social studies. They are titled: TUF (a game of math), Tufabet (a game of words), Origins of World War II (a game of international power politics), Shakespeare, Word Power, Gettysburg, Waterloo, The Stock Market Game, D-Day (World War II invasion game), and Outdoor Survival (a game about wilderness skills). Devised for students whose interest levels range from upper elementary grades through the secondary years, these commercial and educational games (along with some student-produced games) can be incorporated by teachers into their lesson plans.

Student-made games can focus on any subject. For example, the stock market page can be the beginning of an investment adventurer's game. Students can research a company, select a stock to buy and team up to see whose choices paid off. Play money can be used with each team given $1,000 to invest. Terminology relating to the market, pitfalls and benefits of investing money, research on corporations—these are all areas for lesson planning.

In a classroom or in a central library, there should be many action-oriented games which involve students. Games like Scrabble, Life, Monopoly, chess and checkers (all of which encourage concentration) have been around for a long time and are still excellent tools for breaking the monotony of a rigid classroom environment. Many of these games can be used to reinforce vocabulary skills, stress spelling and syllabication (like Scrabble) emphasize decision-making and math skills (Monopoly) or provide exposure to simulated social situations, as in the game of Life.

The "Game Corner" can also become a station for individualized instruction in any subject field. Because students develop educationally at different paces, the audio-tutorial method was developed. This technique, devised by Professor Samuel N. Postlethwait of Purdue University, is an audio-tape teaching approach. It provides each student with an opportunity to operate on his own schedule through a wide range of guided lessons, experiences and additional activities. Self-study cards are sometimes included with cassette-taped lessons. Generally, a study carrel, tape recorder and headset are the basic equipment needed for this approach.

Today, many progressive libraries and media centers house drill tapes and taped lessons, and are equipped with the necessary electronic devices for their use. The tapes can usually be borrowed for a classroom audio-tutorial station or used in the library or materials center, either by individual students or by groups of students. A detailed explanation of Professor Postlethwait's method is explained in *The Audio-Tutorial Approach to Learning: Through Independent Study and Integrated Experiences.* Third edition (Minneapolis, Minnesota: Burgess Publishing Co., 1972).

LET'S GO TO THE MOVIES

Americans indulge in many forms of art. Aside from music and television, movies probably rate highest with teenagers. Taking students on field trips to see movies (or stage plays) that correlate with subjects studied in school has long been an educational practice. Sometimes such a trip is unrelated to the curriculum but is taken simply for entertainment. Entertainment is healthy and can help to establish good teacher-student rapport.

Since film watching is so popular with teens, a teacher can frequently find film aids to teach classroom lessons. For example, in a ten minute film called "Seduction of the Innocent,"[2] teens see how the need to be accepted by a peer group can lead to tragedy. In "Seduction of the Innocent" a teen group "seduces" a young girl into following her urge to try something new. Her standards of right and wrong are clouded by her desire to be accepted by Mike, her boyfriend, and his friends. Although she feels alarm, she goes along, until she and Mike get hooked on heroin.

Films such as this can be shown to stir students to think about their own feelings rather than blindly following their peers in decision making.

Encourage students to discuss the film critically: did it offer an accurate portrayal of people and situations? Turn on the movie projector for ten-minute, seemingly recreational ventures, and you might be able to gradually "turn-on" some teens to a longer attention span.

Besides the school library, an energetic teacher can look into films available from companies and community agencies. Films should not be a gimmick for passing time in the classroom but a strong, motivational tool for learning.

A versatile medium, movies can be considered as an art form, as history and social commentary, as well as a tool for curriculum enrichment. Art has different meaning for different people; however, as a technique, art is usually associated with the making of beautiful objects. Man, as creator, has produced many beautiful things in several artforms (fine arts, language arts, decorative arts, graphic arts and useful arts). His products are frequently both practical and esthetically pleasing.

Movies are one of the newest art forms. Unlike other forms (notably, painting and sculpture), commercial films have to a great extent been a reflection of the tastes and attitudes of the society in which they were filmed. For example, in the past, while society may have viewed the beauty of the naked body from the brush of great painters, it adamantly refused to allow its

---

[2]*Seduction of the Innocent.* (Hollywood, California: Sid Davis Productions, 1961). Color. 10 minutes.

exhibition on the screen. Similarly, it delegated special roles for race, religion, and politics in its presentations. When one traces the development of movies from many of the "oldies" to the present attractions, it becomes apparent that movies are an excellent medium for measuring public opinion. What has been produced on film has been a barometer of what the public wanted as entertainment and what it accepted or rejected—violence, sex, profanity—and has been indicative of changes in these areas.

Movies have also been the vehicle for preserving society's progress as well as its failures through film stories depicting history and projecting what the future may hold. Movies, like books, are great preservers. The film is able to capture and depict a span of time, preserve and hold it for viewing again and again.

One way that children can be taught to appreciate movies as a medium is to teach, as a recreational enterprise, filmmaking and the filming of documentaries. Here again teachers are giving students the opportunity to connect school with "outside" activities, rather than encouraging them to think in isolated terms of what goes on "inside" the school and what goes on "outside" the school.

This medium also offers great possibilities for parent-involvement. Merriam Green, who was going on a Jamaican holiday with her parents at the completion of a "Library-Media Workshop" (see p. 98), was asked to mail back to the teacher a taped letter describing her trip. Every day Merriam was helped by her father to record the data on the tape and describe in detail observations of the ship, the ocean, the harbors, the land, people and their customs, and her general reactions to the trip. She indicated on a map of the West Indies her route from Miami to Port Au Prince, Haiti; to Kingston, Port Antonio and Montego Bay, Jamaica; then back to Miami, Florida (see page 163).

To make the experience even more vivid to her classmates, Merriam made a visual record of the trip. Using an 8mm movie camera, Merriam and her father were able to document the vacation as they went along. The film coincided with the taped account.

Students in social studies followed with interest their classmate's descriptions of the inhabitants of Haiti and Jamaica, their bargaining tactics, their arts and crafts projects; the flow of traffic

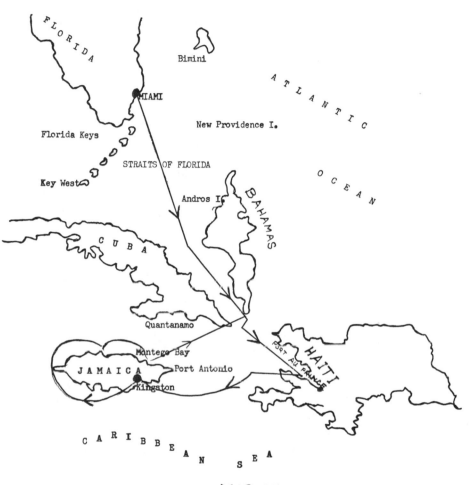

MAP OF WEST INDIES

through the streets in a seemingly haphazard way; tours of industrial and residential sections, scenic gardens; descriptions of various cities and a comparison of these to her hometown.

One student's experience with film making demonstrated to others how versatile and effective movies could be in conveying information and feelings, and in creating beautiful images.

MUSICAL IMAGES

The eyes and ears of today's students perceive a totally different world from that of their ancestors. As McLuhan noted in *The Medium is the Massage,* "We are enveloped by sound. It forms a seamless web around us. We say, 'Music shall fill the air.' We never say, 'Music shall fill a particular segment of the air.' "[3]

The sounds of music *do* fill the air all around us. We hear it over dishwasher hum and shower flow. It blasts through radio and television sets to accompany voices expounding the virtues of commercial products. Music of every description pours forth around us no matter where we are. Teens have developed their own distinct sounds through rock, folk, jazz and soul groups. The more popular groups who have hit the "smash record" status keep the music industry grinding records out by the millions annually.

Many of the sounds which the young groups are producing today have very powerful messages. They sing about love, about the drug scene, about brotherhood and sisterhood, about ghetto life and hard times, about moral and political issues. They provide the teacher in search of curriculum ideas with a medium and messages to which teens are certain to relate. Music as a communicative art can be expanded from the study of Bach, Beethoven and Brahms to: an extra-curricular activity club; a dynamic recreation activity; a mini-course for young people interested in music performance; or, as a summer-long independent or individualized study and work project.

In the music classroom the examination and critical discernment of "bad" rock, rhythm and blues or soul music can provide the music student with motivation to study music more seriously.

---

[3]Marshall McLuhan and Quentin Fiore, *The Medium Is the Massage* (New York: Random House, 1967), p. 111.

For others, teachers can still capitalize on the music involvement of their students.

The teacher who incorporates jazz or country music in the classroom will learn (as well as teach) a great deal from his or her students about the meaning of popular music.

Some Projects Centering on Music

1. Collect stories about your favorite music group.
2. Make posters of your favorite group.
3. Clip pictures; make scrapbooks, collages, or frame photographs you've sent for and received.
4. Study the stories behind show business success: Who writes the entertainers' songs? Who gave them their first inspiration?
5. Study and interpret the lyrics of one of your favorite songs.
6. Choose a style of music: blues, gospel, secular or sacred music; jazz, folk, popular, classical, chamber, opera. Write the lyrics for a song using one or more of the headings.
7. Find a poem on a similar topic; compare the song you have written with the poem.
8. Write a short rock opera like "Tommy" by the Who. Create music, lyrics and drama. Produce it; videotape the production.
9. Conduct a music workshop, utilizing local talent to explain how to select and buy musical instruments; how to play guitars and electric pianos, make a dub, distribute records, select a manager or promoter; plan and write publicity and advertising. Learn about putting on a show; copyrighting music; royalties for song writers, performers, arrangers, producers; joining a union as a musician or performer, etc.
10. Write an essay on "The Way We Live, as Expressed in Music."
11. Play a record or a tape; write a poem, essay or story, draw a cartoon or picture expressing your emotional reaction to the record or tape played.
12. Refer to music and record criticism in the entertainment section of a magazine or newspaper. Pull out descriptive words and research their meanings, words such as improvisation, crescendo, theme and variations, rythm, melody, harmony, tempo. Allow students to enlarge this list, explaining the meanings of words they add.
13. Research information on the ratio between groups aspiring to "make it in show business" and those actually achieving fame and fortune.

14. Pretend you are managing a group. Construct a contract which could be used in consummating arrangements for performances. (A sample follows.)

CONTRACT

STATE OF INDIANA

ss

COUNTY OF LAKE

AGREEMENT

THIS AGREEMENT, entered into this ＿＿day of ＿＿＿＿＿＿ , 197＿＿ by and between Ms. Josephine Doe, manager of the DYNAMIC FIVE (a vocal and instrumental music group in Gary, Indiana), and ＿＿＿＿＿＿

＿＿＿＿＿＿＿＿＿＿＿＿＿＿＿＿＿＿＿＿＿＿＿＿＿

the parents or legal guardians of ＿＿＿＿＿＿＿＿＿＿＿
(a minor, who is a member of the DYNAMIC FIVE).

All parties herewith agree that, from the date of this contract, Ms. Doe shall serve as manager for one year and shall hold a year's option to renew that agreement, for handling all recording, radio, television, and public appearances, both foreign and domestic, of the DYNAMIC FIVE.

It is agreed that in consideration for her services Ms. Doe will be paid a management fee of twenty per cent (20%) of whatever rates are agreed upon by the manager and promoters.

The parties hereto have read the foregoing terms and conditions and believe the same to be fair and reasonable, and accordingly have affixed their hands and seals this ＿＿＿day of ＿＿＿＿＿＿ , 197＿＿ .

By:＿＿＿＿＿＿＿＿＿＿＿＿   ＿＿＿＿＿＿＿＿＿＿＿＿＿
Ms. Josephine Doe, Manager   Self, Parent or Legal Guardian

Address   (Spouse)

City   State   Zip   Address

＿＿＿＿＿＿＿＿＿＿＿＿＿＿   City   State   Zip
NOTARY PUBLIC

My Commission Expires:

WHAT DO YOU THINK?

Teen-agers like to voice their opinions about things: their favorite movie stars; their political, religious or moral convictions; boy-girl relationships; child-adult conflicts; their favorite vocal and instrumental music groups; education and discipline. However, too few opportunities are provided for them to develop adequate skills in oral expression. Students may learn the rudiments of public speaking in a speech class, but rarely do they have opportunities to develop good discussion and conversation techniques. Perhaps, the emphasis has been too much on the reading of assignments, workbook completion, or simply supplying monosyllabic or fragmentary answers to questions raised by teachers. As a consequence, when students are forced into situations which require good verbal expression they may feel inadequate, timid or ashamed to express themselves.

Did you ever think of allowing students to hold rap sessions as a part of a classroom communications activity? Let the class vote on a topic for discussion from several choices. Then divide the class into two groups. Let one side ask the questions, the other side provide answers. Allow as many opinions to be expressed as possible. Or, as a second choice, let students write down questions on any topic which they would like to have their classmates consider. Drop the questions in a hat, allowing each student to pick a question and voice his honest opinion concerning the question asked.

If you think the questions and answers are newsworthy, keep a tape recorder handy and ask students to transcribe and edit what is good. Then, publish a "Rapping 'Round Newsheet" periodically to keep the interest flowing. This is also a good way to improve students' skills in transmitting oral to written communication. Good sentence structure, spelling, creative expression, punctuation, voice inflection, should all be used in constructing questions and in giving responses.

Students might construct a collage of photographs of famous writers. Each picture can be numbered, then later identified by members of the class. In a very relaxed mood, students may discuss the lives of the writers, talk about their significant literary works, or relate passages they particularly enjoyed. Perhaps they would enjoy constructing a large map of the United States where they can write in authors' names, titles of literature, and special literary events according to their importance to particular cities and states. Also, students could trace trends in literature as they reflect society's thinking, historical facts, and political leadership of a period.

The social studies teacher may encourage students to construct a map of the United States on a sheet of paper which covers a large wall area of the classroom. Call it the "Graffiti Sheet of Historical Data." Students can record historical facts on the sheet, placing the record in its proper city and state, and dating it when necessary (for example: The first President to be assassinated was Abraham Lincoln, April 14, 1865—an entry which would be placed in Washington, D.C. on the map). Students may use a variety of colored pencils or felt-tipped markers for their entries.

The "Graffiti Sheet" might make an excellent topic for discussion as well as for test questions or quizzes. In addition to the textbook, newspapers and magazines, the recorded entries may be pulled from *The Lincoln Library of Essential Information* (Buffalo, N.Y.: Frontier Press, 1971) or from almanacs such as *The World Almanac and Book of Facts, Information Please Almanac,* or other publications supplying either historical data or current information.

PLAN SUCCESSFUL FIELD TRIPS

Field trips need not be expensive or complicated. Sometimes a stroll through a beautiful park, a scenic bus trip or a bus ride to the "other side of the tracks," a walk to a nearby shrine, a visit to a neighboring school, a library or other public building can provide an orientation or culmination to a unit, and help students become aware of their surroundings.

Consider "ordinary" topics which can be built into interesting field trips: ecology, pollution, photography, conservation of natural resources, community pride and beautification, urban revitalization—many topics which fill the local newspapers with information about community growth and development can be utilized within the classroom. Let students select trip possibilities. Emphasize the desire to correlate the type of trip with the current lesson.

For example, let us assume the lesson topic relates to community revitalization. Research information about an area proposed for revitalization. Clip pictures from newspapers and magazines depicting "before," and "after" portrayals of blighted areas which have been renewed. Cut out pictures from newspapers and magazines depicting how you would like your own community to look were the residents to become involved in a rehabilitation program. Construct dioramas, mountings, posters, collages, etc. suggesting how your community would look if it were involved in its own revitalization. Research films and filmstrips relating to the topic; show these before and after the field trip. Allow students to photograph "before" and "after" scenes with their own cameras. Choose areas which the class may visit: one area to suggest the need for revitalization, another area showing what has been done. Invite city personnel to give lectures, conduct workshops, distribute brochures. Correlate career possibilities with the field trip.

Some Inexpensive Field Trips

1. Visit a nearby college, university, technical or career institution.
2. Make a trip to the public library, a special library in the area, or a regional library.
3. Tour a nearby fire station, political convention, municipal court, police station, county courthouse, a civic center.
4. Observe (by special permission) the workings of a local bank, credit union, currency exchange.
5. Tour a local business or industry.
6. View the developments at a construction project for community improvement.
7. Visit the local zoo, park, museum, shrine, historic landmark.
8. Tour a nearby airport, planetarium, terrarium, etc.
9. Visit a farm, beach, amusement center.
10. Take a "gourmet treat tour" to a foreign restaurant: French, Chinese, Italian, Japanese, Greek, etc.
11. Spend a day in a wilderness retreat at a Girl or Boy Scout camp site.

12. Visit a religious ceremony (wedding, holiday festival, seasonal celebration, or other special observance).
13. Attend a naturalization ceremony at the courthouse.

CORRELATE AFTER-SCHOOL ACTIVITIES WITH CLASSWORK

Since students engage in a number of extra-curricular activities after school and when the school year has ended, the innovative teacher can capitalize on these activities with assignments that utilize community resources to correlate reading and multi-media techniques with the school program.

"Book Bingo" is a fascinating game played by children engaged in the 1974 Summer Reading program of the Gary Public Library.[4] The game provided excellent motivation for reading throughout the summer months. "Book Bingo" embraced the element of chance as the traditional Bingo game does, and not only provided a built-in motivational force for increasing reading skills, but also increased the circulation statistics for the public library in general. This idea, which is adaptable to school library programs and reading classes (especially on the elementary, intermediate and middle schools levels), is explained in detail in the following paragraphs.

A registration sheet containing the child's name, school and grade for the coming year was kept at each branch library. A membership card was given to each participant as he registered, and each was provided with a Bingo card (page 171).

As books were read, the participants returned to the library and drew a numbered disc from the Bingo shaker. If one of the numbers appearing on the card was selected, the entrants were allowed to write into each matching square the titles of the books read. If this space was already filled, the participant could draw again. Bingo was obtained in the usual fashion of the game by a completed vertical, horizontal or diagonal line or four corners.

A hole was punched in the membership card issued to each participant to provide an immediate count of the number of books he or she had read in the Summer Reading Program (page 172).

---

[4]Created by Mrs. Ana Maria Grandfield; Librarian, Gary Public Library, Gary, Indiana.

NAME- Last Name First

SCHOOL   Grade just completed

Book Bingo

BINGO

B	I	N	G	O
The Time Machine 17		Leslie 3/1	5/1	That Was Then, This Is Now 7/1
2	28	Kings of Motor Speed 4/2	The Witch of Blackbird Pond 5/2	6/2
Count Me Gone 3	2/3	FREE	5/3	7/3
Don't Look and It Won't Hurt 4/4	Classmates by Request 2/4	40	The Year 2000 5/4	Adopted Jane 6/4
5	2/5	Look Before You Leap 3/5	50	Jean and Johnny 4/5

GARY PUBLIC LIBRARY

_____ BRANCH

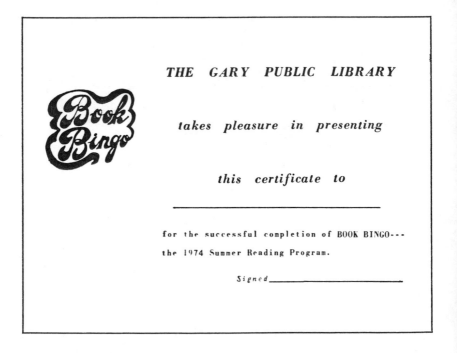

This procedure was followed until the participant "Bingo-ed." Then he was rewarded with a certificate for the first completed game of Bingo. The second-time winner and winners thereafter were rewarded with gift-wrapped prizes from a "Grab Bag." A new Book Bingo card was issued and participants would proceed to try to Bingo again. The program lasted throughout the summer. The names of Book Bingo winners were posted on a large, painted wheel provided for that purpose at each library branch.

A brief book report form can be established by the teacher to encourage the critical examination and analysis of books read upon completion of the program.

8

Arousing Students' Interest in the Environment

Even though we live in a technologically advanced age, it is obvious that we don't think any faster than in less sophisticated times. Too frequently we teach about today and yesterday and fail to encourage students to project their ideas into the future. Now on the threshold of a new century, we need to think about the next 100 or more years. An effort to anticipate the future in light of our past and present is vital, and a study of man's relationship to his environment, projected into the next century, can be a valuable approach to teaching science, social consciousness and communicative skills.

In the winter of 1973, millions of Americans had their first personal exposure to the inconveniences of the energy squeeze. They experienced lowered temperatures in schools, in homes, and in business establishments. On the highways, service stations closed on Sundays and sometimes during the week. There were fewer Christmas tree lights and lighted holiday displays in front of homes and businesses.

Americans are becoming more aware that waterways and airways are being polluted. Favorite fishing spots have no fish but contain oily residues, worn out tires and other junk. In some places in the United States, people have begun wearing face masks to breathe easier in thick smog.

Newspapers, magazines, journals—all have had an abundance of articles on citizens' groups fighting against decisions to erect nuclear energy plants near favorite recreation areas, insisting on pollution abatement measures, monitoring neighboring waterways for dumping, participating in public hearings to encourage continued efforts to protect our earth.

Young persons as well as old are ready for a deeper, more personal response to the nations's environmental problems. Earth, water, air, energy—these are the common heritage of mankind and we want to maintain these elements of life at a high level. In educating students we want to convey the importance of respecting nature as well as each other. Also, we can project the process whereby a high quality of life is transferred with full vitality from one generation to another. The intent in these projects is to refresh students' affection for nature and to make clear their responsibility in preserving our earth while enjoying its bounties.

Our future can become what we conceive it to be. "Playing it by ear" or drifting into change is the result of a philosophy that we are too helpless to do otherwise. However, we are not victims. We can be in charge of our destiny. We can project the future to be enjoyed by our descendants. In their turn, our descendants will develop projects by which to maintain our earth and our good quality of life.

Students can understand living as well as literature and history. A caring teacher in any classroom can guide teens to balance their quest for pleasure, power, and material gain with the need to preserve nature and respect society. Through classroom assignments that reject mediocrity and comformity and support their convictions about "earthkeeping," students and teachers can take positive steps toward environmental health and well being.

IGNORANCE POLLUTES THE ENVIRONMENT: LEARNING ABOUT ECOLOGY

Population, technology and industrialization plus a passive attitude toward the conservation of natural resources—these are the main causes of environmental pollution. Human beings have psychological as well as biological necessities: quiet, privacy, independence, opportunities for initiative, and open spaces. For want of these necessities they become stressful.

> The gross national product runs to 900 billion dollars a year and includes producing nuclear weapons, polluting air, fighting crime. As Robert Kennedy observed... "it measures everything, in short, except that which makes life worthwhile."[1]

To begin lifting the fog about pollution and how our quality of life is altered by the stresses of change and choice in society, a teacher can use varied instructional aids in the classroom.

One such aid is the atlas *The Earth and Man*[2] that expresses a "down to earth" view of man's magnificent natural inheritance. This volume provides a pictorial guide to the earth's resources and the relationship of man to the natural elements of life. The section on what turns man's waste into pollution (from pages 134-142) explores 48 specifics including pinpointing on a map of a city how pollutants emitted from everywhere produce unwanted by-products that the environment has a difficult time accommodating. A few pages in each of these sections "The Abuse of the Earth," "Pathways of Pollution," "Controlling Pollution," and "Man the Aggressor" are easy-to-follow, awareness-building, pictorial guides to how man has been beguiled into believing that his resources are endless.

Some heavenly space photographs of earth in the section "Earth from Space" on pages 20-23 are awe inspiring. As Neil Armstrong, an American astronaut observed, "Earth looks like a beautiful jewel in space."[3]

In this illustrated encyclopedia of earth phonomena, a teacher can find pictures and commentary to provoke interest and further study of man and his environment. Using the overhead

---

[1]Herbert J. Muller, *The Children of Frankenstein; a Primer on Modern Technology and Human Values* (Bloomington, Ind.: Indiana University Press, 1970), p. 12.

[2]*The Earth and Man; a Rand McNally World Atlas.* (New York: Rand McNally and Co., 1972).

[3]*Ibid.*, p. 20.

projector, the instructor or interested student can pinpoint specifics and students can better understand technical materials.

Overhead transparency sets along with filmstrips on issues such as air and water pollution include visual information that promotes quick relays of the scope and complexities of the problems. Two such sets which provide basic information are: *Air Pollution* and *Water Pollution,* produced by the Scott Education Division in Holyoke, Massachusetts, 1970. Each set contains nine transparencies, 23 overlays and two filmstrips with records or cassettes. The topics included are increasing urbanization, the costs of air and water pollution, the responsibilities of lobbies, what we can do as private citizens, primary and secondary waste treatment systems, and "the greenhouse effect" (when carbon dioxide builds up and traps solar heat within the atmoshpere).

An excellent film for the teacher to use is *Future Shock,*[4] which constantly bombards us with the theme: too much change arrived at too quickly causes devastating effects. Orson Wells provides the commentary on people's sense of always being on the move—"Home is a place to leave"; the family that traditionally provided comfort and security has become more mobile, less dependable; and many other social and political super-changes have occurred. Technological strengths are defined as shock creators because of their wide ranging impact on society.

To prevent "future shock," the film urges us to question our present value system and to think about the kinds of choices necessary for the future. After viewing the film, students may discuss and write about the controversial ideas presented.

Say No! is a nifty book that the author, Ruth Adams, calls a guide to action to save our environment.[5] Ask groups within the class to report on chapters such as "Our Air Is an Unlicensed Dump," "Water's Too Precious to Foul," "How to Save Trees for a Greener Future," "The Silent Minority (Animals) on This Planet."

---

[4]Based on the book by Alvin Toffler (New York: McGraw Hill, 1973). 16mm color. 42 minutes.

[5]Ruth Adams, *Say No! The New Pioneers' Guide to Action to Save Our Environment* (Emmaus, Pennsylvania: Rodale Press, Inc., 1971).

Here is straightforward writing that is easy to understand. Case studies and anecdotes relate how groups have acted against what may have appeared to be short-term benefits.

Examples of letters written by Ruth Adams pinpoint problems such as polystyrene egg cartons which give off phosgene, a "nerve gas," when burned; disposable baby needs such as blankets, shirts, furniture which intensify solid waste problems; the health hazards of chemical food additives. She wrote to those responsible for the problems.

Students can be urged to submit similar letters to those who are in a position to bring about change. Generate interest in such letter writing by calling attention to "the voice of the people" section of the local newspaper.

BUILDING ENVIRONMENTAL AWARENESS

Community Renewal

●Encourage students to turn a critical eye toward their community and their immediate neighborhoods. Notice rubbish, untidyness, disrespect for neighbors' property, lack of pride in one's own property, etc. Ask students to write about their observations and include suggestions for cleaning up their environment. Tie in a class project on ecology to coincide with local beautification drives, clean-up week or national "Earth Day." Before and after the drive, pictures may be taken showing how students attacked community sites and helped to beautify them.

●Ask students to bring in photographs of poverty stricken areas. As they focus on them they are to name the objects in the picture (broken down fences, vacant lots, boarded up houses, playgrounds, parks,) which identify the condition of the neighborhood. Who are the people? What are they doing—loitering? working? playing? What could the people do to improve their area? Suggest activities such as these:

> Write a theme on how you would like to see this area improved.
> Write a poem or a play portraying residents in this area.
> Draw a poster about what you see.

●Encourage students to focus on recreation areas in their community. Ask them to take pictures, sketch favorite sites and write about them. Place this information in a class scrapbook.

Include original poems in the scrapbook. Here is an example of one student's work:

WE'LL KNOW THE EARTH'S POLLUTED
We'll know the earth's polluted
Polluted beyond repair
When the snow turns black
Falling from the air;
When the clouds turn green
Like a fungus in the sky
And the sun becomes red,
As if dipped in dye;
When the earth rots away
Right under our feet
And the world burns away
From a blast of solar heat.

—*Valerie Thompson, grade 8*

Endangered Species

In *The Earth and Man* (pp. 86-87), the section on endangered animals pictures the vicuna, polar bear, audouin's gull, the whooping crane and other species endangered by human exploitation. Students can research the reasons some animals are on the endangered list. They can bring in articles about city facilities on animal care and control. The health department and animal shelter personnel can be invited to discuss their responsibilities and what the public's responsibilities should be.

Natural causes of death, uncontrolled hunters, habitat destruction and disturbance are briefly described as the reasons for endangered animals. Many students have pets and have a special joy in touching animals, owning animals, and loving them. Their natural interest can be sparked to a protective interest.

Language arts teachers can spur the reluctant reader to explore books such as *May I Keep This Clam, Mother? It Followed Me Home,* by naturalist Ronald Rood, which is filled with anecdotes about finding unusual pets and taking care of them.[6] Easy-to-read materials that also convey a thoughtful message and appeal to young teens are constantly being published. Our respon-

---

[6]Ronald Rood, *May I Keep This Clam, Mother? It Followed Me Home.* (New York: Simon and Schuster, 1973).

sibility as teachers with foresight is to discover them and introduce them to our students.

Land Use and Abuse

Students can trace how, through improved shelter and food gathering techniques, people have caused pollution of the earth. The use of land involves environmental control. There are usually penalties for abuse. Students can trace prehistoric patterns of society, the beginning of agriculture, the medieval use of land, the industrial revolution, and modern land use.

Conservation

Forests are being depleted and waste paper prices are escalating. A paper drive is an environmentally and economically sound project. Students' efforts to collect paper and sell it for reuse can lead to productive learning.

Controlling Noise

Preserving and transmitting sound over distances has implemented world wide communication, but has also resulted in accompanying noise pollution. Sound is a form of energy that must be controlled. Noise is unwanted sound. At what point does usefulness turn into disturbance? In a machine-oriented society, high levels of noise can create anxiety and annoyance. Teens' music can be disturbing to some; to others, absolute silence can be horrifying. Usually the sounds we make don't bother us, but— what about the other guy?

Social studies teachers can supplement textbooks on sound with environmental protection materials and can teach students how the government helps to protect citizens from noise nuisances. An examination of regulations, local codes and ordinances that deal with noise abuse and noise abatement can be educationally sound.

In language arts class, students can write about noise. Encourage the use of descriptive words that conjure up pictures such as screeching jets, rumbling trucks, blaring rock music, grinding motors of huge machines.

High stress noise level is an important argument against constructing new airports. Ask students to examine one airport conflict in a metropolitan area. Use the *Reader's Guide to Periodical Literature* to find recent articles that explain the pros and cons of the crisis. Examine these questions related to the building of the airport: (1) Will natural areas be destroyed? (2) Will new jobs be created? (3) Will there be more air pollution? (4) Will the noise level increase? (5) Will the airport provide a transportation convenience for the community?

Historic Preservation

Every state has its interesting places and significant historical sites. Researching such a site can help students understand another way an environment can be enriched.

Pictorial guides to community structures can be prepared by students with cameras. Also, the class might invite an architect, archeologist, or historian to discuss the value of preserving the past as a way to introduce these careers.

A good resource book for the teacher and the students who are aware of cultural landmarks is *Lost America* by Constance Grieff.[7] Grieff presents a pictorial guide to the disappearance of America's architectural heritage—valuable buildings that might have been maintained but now can never be recouped.

ANALYZING ISSUES: DRAMATIC ACTION

One value of drama lies in its reflection of man's social environment. As such, it becomes an effective vehicle for use in the classroom to depict conflicts and work out solutions. Thus dramatics provide an especially useful tool for use in ecology lessons.

Students in language arts and social studies classes can use role-playing techniques in setting up a mock public hearing in the classroom to explore some of the following conflicts: People want clean air, yet they need to keep their jobs at a plant that pollutes the air. Blight may kill trees in the city, but residents object to paying higher taxes which the city needs if it is to replant trees to keep the air clean and the environment more beautiful. City noises cause stress but seem necessary to communication. Natural areas,

---

[7]Constance M. Greiff, ed. *Lost America; From the Atlantic to the Mississippi* (Princeton: The Pyne Press, 1971).

such as the dunes and prairies in Indiana, provide play areas and rich natural history, yet they are slowly being excavated while citizens' groups struggle to preserve them. Passenger trains make no new demands on our diminishing land area and create a negligible amount of pollution. Because they are less profitable, however, the federal government does not spend as much to maintain their services as they do on the airlines.

After students investigate these conflicts and decide where their priorities lie, they can begin to understand different points of view and special interest in environmental decision making. They can dramatize this information as proponents and observers in a mock public hearing.

Part of the class would be the objective hearing committee. Perhaps they could represent the Commission on the Status of Environmental Protection. They would prepare some questions and answers related to the testimony of their classmates. Some of the class members would be active participants who have selected a point of view and present testimony to support their position. The rest of the class would be the audience. Some members of the audience would listen carefully and prepare summaries of the testimony of the witnesses at the hearing. If possible, students should be encouraged to attend an actual public hearing taking place in the community.

Groups of students can also dramatize a corporate meeting of "top brass" decision makers discussing pollution abatement, workers' health, and strategies for coping with outraged citizen groups calling for immediate changes within the plant.

To understand the question of priorities, students can dramatize an ecology club meeting of citizens opposed to a water safety measure involving cholorine handling and a proposal for a shopping center that would destroy a wooded area in a densely populated neighborhood.

The students and teacher would decide on the time limits and other ground rules for testimony and discussion so that many students would get a chance to participate in each of these activities.

PROJECTS, CHALLENGES, STRATEGIES AND ACTIVITIES

What are some of the challenges to which our students must be alerted? First, we must become alert to the environment in our own communities. For example, many years ago the children would see the hazy grey-red sky above the mills of Gary, Indiana, and remark, "Wow! Look at the mill dust and smoke!" Now, children observe that sign of air pollution with concern and are joining adults in asking for improvements to abate those life-zapping fumes and dust. With laws encouraging them, industries are beginning procedures to clean up their wastes so that people can enjoy clean air and see the sun and a blue sky once more.

All ills of society are said to be solved by education. While educators may feel overwhelmed by their responsibility at times, students can develop the ability to make decisions based on thought-through factual information, a pattern of thought and behavior that can benefit themselves and society.

Project 1
Correlate Fact and Fiction

Reading assignments for gathering information can be geared to non-fiction materials. All too frequently the emphasis in reading is on entertainment. Teachers can help students build a sense of community pride and environmental interest by introducing non-fiction and fictional reading materials that educate students about survival issues. Data collecting for survival needs could lead to better control of their destiny.

Things to Do

Assign reading materials about life in the twenty-first century. These appeal to the sense of wonder and adventure that teens possess. Include suggestions such as these:

Bell, Daniel, ed. *Toward the Year 2000: Work in Progress*. Boston: Houghton Mifflin, 1968.

Drucker, Peter F. *The Age of Discontinuity: Guidelines to Our Changing Society.* New York: Harper & Row, 1969.

Fromm, Erich. *The Revolution of Hope: Toward a Humanized Technology*. New York: Harper & Row, 1968.

Harrison, Harry, ed. *The Year 2000; an Anthology*. Garden City, New York: Doubleday, 1970.

Hellman, Hal. *The City in the World of the Future*. New York: M. Evans and Co., 1970

Huxley, Aldous. *Brave New World*. New York: Harper & Row, 1932.

Huxley, Aldous. *Brave New World Revisited*. New York: Harper & Row, 1959.

Katep, George. *Utopia and Its Enemies.* Glencoe, Illinois: Free Press, 1963.

Schwartz, Alvin. *Old Cities and New Towns; the Changing Face of the Nation.* New York: E.P. Dutton & Co., 1968.

Toffler, Alvin. *Future Shock.* New York: Random House, 1970.

Project 2
A Twenty-First Century
Interplanetary Fantasy

Fantasize a voyage to another planet in the twenty-first century. The intent of this unit is to have fun imagining an interplanetary voyage, describing plant and animal life on another planet, and being creative and innovative while learning to project futuristic thoughts.

Things to Do

Simulate a diary of your voyage; keep a daily record of events. Draw a map representing your destination. Describe the space ship in which you will travel. What does its interior look like? What are the special features of the vehicle? Feel free to describe the electronic devices on the space ship. Indicate where your spaceship will land. Mark significant landmarks of the planet: water areas, mountain areas, wooded areas, flat lands, etc.

Include answers to questions such as these: (1.) What are the new sources for energy? (2.) What kinds of packaged foods would you take with you? (3.) Describe the existence of life on the planet: vegetation? animal life? waterways? atmosphere? (4.) Will you be equipped with any kinds of technological gear to breathe, to see, or get around on this planet? Describe. (5.) What national symbols will you take to this new planet? Why would you select these symbols? How will you use them?

Project 3
Focusing on the City

Next, ask students to focus on controversial environmental concerns in their own city. Class discussions can lead to awareness building of how man creates some of his own problems.

Things to Do

Ask students to probe for a better understanding and a perspective on how they can be part of the answer to problems of living in a harmonious community. Center the discussion on problems such as these: Assume that you have been asked what we can do to prevent garbage being dumped in our parks and neighborhoods. How can you stop littering?

Can you determine who is telling half-truths and who is telling the truth when a citizens' group points an accusing finger at a utility company beginning to build a nuclear reactor plant? The citizens say that they will face dire health consequences from such an energy plant. The company says that the nuclear reactor will prevent "brown outs" and take care of energy needs vital to enjoying modern conveniences. What approach would you use in discussing this problem and in acting to protect the environment? Follow this discussion with a written assignment.

Write an analysis of the issues involved in reaching an understanding of these citizen concerns.

Then focus on other citizen concerns with probing questions like these: (1) Is the city designed around people's conveniences? (Many cities are no longer so designed, especially quickly built suburban areas.) (2) How much time and energy is spent in going from home to work and school and back again? (3) Are the parks, libraries, churches and school playgrounds used and enjoyed or are they merely symbols of a wealthy society no longer in touch with nature and peace of spirit? (4) Are streams and trees and old significant structures preserved as amenities or as obstacles to progress?

Assist students in planning the renewal of one square block of the city to be torn down and rebuilt consistent with ideas of how they want their block to be in the future. Plan (according to mathematical dimensions) the whole square block: include placement of buildings, utilities and transportation routes which may be underground or overhead, open recreation sites, and landscaping.

Project 4
Planning for People

In *The Earth and Man*, a transition from landscape to townscape is pictorially presented showing rural America and urban America. Service institutions, play areas, dwellings, industries are traced in their growth and development. In a social studies class on urban and community problems, students can discuss the planning or lack of planning that they perceive in their own city's development. What kind of renewal is taking place, if any? Also, students may reflect on the many diverse influences that create communities which do not serve the best needs of their members.

Using a grid outline of a well-known city such as Chicago, students can study the network of recreational and work areas, living quarters, waterways, airways and other transportational provisions planned for people. The community grid creates a vehicle for drawing generalizations about land use planning. For example, the grid project might provide a theme for classroom discussion on topics such as the effects of crowding on personalities, jobs, and community services. What does the flight of people to the suburbs mean to the inner city dweller and to suburban dwellers? (See page 187.)

Things to Do

To illustrate the problem of city zoning and planning for growth and change, ask students to simulate their community by filling in the grid outline with the work places of their parents, major business and industrial sites, recreation areas, their school, park areas, waterways, shopping areas they frequent, their church, special friends' homes.

Then on another grid pattern ask them to simulate a community that is more conveniently set out. They can use a color guide as a key to areas indicated.

Questions to focus on the community are: (1) Would you include more parks, recreation areas in a community? (2) How would you lay out plans for better residential areas? (3) Would you provide for large apartment dwellings and one family dwellings? (4) Is there adequate public transportation from one site to another? (5) Should different land uses be kept separate? (6) Should every community have industry? shopping centers? cultural facilities? open spaces? (7) How do citizens regulate and influence development? (8) Are taxes assessed on personal property?

(9) What kind of public transportation is available to get from one neighborhood to another? What kind of transportation does your family use? (10) How can you and your family conserve on fuel? (11) What does the lay-out of a city have to do with fuel conservation?

(12) What kind of development is taking place in your community, if any? (13) How are school boundaries determined? city limits? neighborhoods? (14) Are there diverse recreational facilities in good condition nearby? *Explain and discuss your observations.*

Project 5
Enjoying Nature Through a Mini-Garden

Wonder in growing things and in enjoying the natural environment can be taught within a language arts class. Teachers

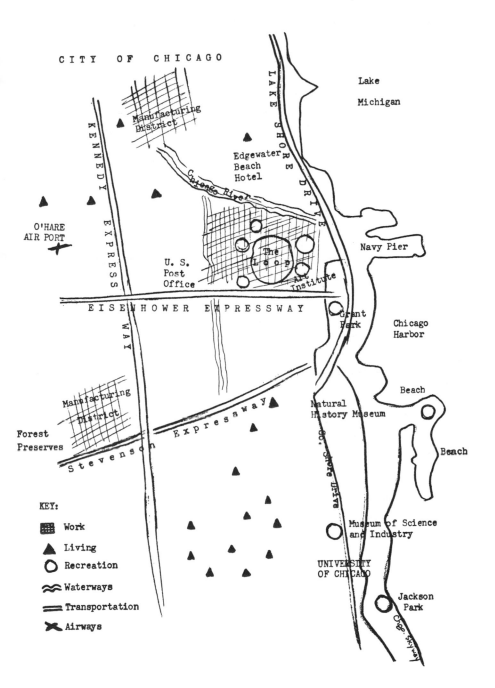

CITY OF CHICAGO

Manufacturing District

Edgewater Beach Hotel

Lake Michigan

Chicago River

O'HARE AIR PORT

U. S. Post Office

The Loop

Art Institute

Navy Pier

Grant Park

Chicago Harbor

EISENHOWER EXPRESSWAY

Manufacturing District

Stevenson Expressway

Forest Preserves

Beach

Natural History Museum

Beach

Museum of Science and Industry

UNIVERSITY OF CHICAGO

Jackson Park

KEY:

Work

Living

Recreation

Waterways

Transportation

Airways

can initiate reading and writing assignments that encourage students to internalize the point that each student is an "earthkeeper".

Things to Do

An assignment that stresses reading for directions, following them and seeing the results can be structured around growing interesting houseplants from seeds and pits of fruits and vegetables. Such a project, centered around a book such as *The After Dinner Gardening Book*, not only orients reading lessons but also potentiates other environmental understanding for students.[8]

A mini-garden can be part of the effort to build respect for living things and to emphasize the balance of life through sun, water, and earth. This activity extends the zest for the natural green environment. This simple interaction of students and nature also beautifies the classroom surroundings.

Using human energy in growing our own food, as in walking and cycling, is satisfying, exhilarating, and healthful. Teachers must help young persons transcend limitations of habit as socialized human beings and liberate their bodies and minds in self-propelled activities.

Project 6
Environmental Activism

Environmentalists can be invited to discuss their goals and strategies with students. Ecology-oriented challenges can be mind-opening as a way to begin exploring jobs that make a difference in a community.

Students can also be encouraged to participate in the grass roots movement for changes. Conservation organizations are eager to share materials and to gain supporters in their efforts to maintain a healthy environment. Timely, inspiring, and thought-provoking materials are available on things to know and to do about water, air, noise pollution; pesticides, sewage and waste disposal; wildlife protection; land use controls, transportation needs population, and aesthetic concerns.

Things to Do

Letter writing activities can strengthen students' skills in written communication and also encourage students to use

---

[8]Richard W. Langer, *The After-Dinner Gardening Book* (Toronto, Canada: Macmillian Co., 1969).

the mails to gain information and to share information. They can write to the following environmental activists for information:

1. Common Cause; 2100 N St., N.W.; Washington, D.C. 20037.

   (This is a national citizen's lobby which focuses on change and reform in many subject areas. There may be a representative of this organization in your vicinity.)

2. League of Women Voters of the U.S.; 1730 M St., N.W.; Washington, D.C. 20036

   (There are many local Leagues whose members could be consulted on the feasibility of an environmental project and whether the League can be supportive of it. Also, this is an informed, non-partisan group of persons whom you might consider inviting to speak on other relevant, local issues.)

3. Sierra Club; 1050 Mills Tower; San Francisco, California 94104

   (There are state organizations throughout the country.)

4. National Aududon Society; 1130 Fifth Avenue; New York City, N. Y. 10028.

5. National Wildlife Federation; 1412 16th Street, N.W.; Washington, D.C. 20036.

6. Ask for a listing of inexpensive and free government materials from:

   The Superintendent of Documents; U.S. Government Printing Office; Washington, D.C. 20402.

Students can also write for more information and direction to The Center for Science in the Public Interest, 1779 Church Street, N.W. Washington, D.C. 20036. C.S.P.I. is a non-profit, tax exempt organization which advocates that science and technology be responsibe to human needs.

WHAT IF. . .

Set out hypothetical problems of conservation. Ask students to decide on meaningful actions to cope with shortages such as those suggested below. (Each student is to write a paragraph indicating his or her feeling about the crisis before explaining the plan of action.)

1. If gas were rationed to 30 gallons a week and you had a job requiring 40 gallons to get to work and back home each week. . .
   How would you conserve gas?

2 If oil deliveries were curtailed and you heat your home with oil. . .
    What would you do to conserve oil?

3. If the airlines cut their weekly round-trip flights between London and Chicago by a third but the company you work for required you to work closely with agents in London. . .
    What would you do?

4. If periodic "rolling blackouts" left your home without power for periods of time. . .
    How would you cope?

5. If paper sacks were not distributed at the grocery store. . .
    How might you conserve reusable materials?

6. If the price of beef zoomed 50% higher a pound and you had three young children to feed. . .
    What would you substitute?

7. If your water supply were limited each month. . .
    How would you conserve water?

Encourage students to think through an approach to a local industrially-provoked environmental problem. For example, what if a corporation decides that it will relocate in another state rather then invest in pollution-abatement machinery to handle emission from old equipment. People will be out of work if this happens. Some town waterways will be cleaned up because waste materials from the corporation's plant will no longer exist. Also, the air will be cleaner because the smoke from the plant will have disappeared. Weigh the benefits and costs of a specific clean-up program.

PETITIONING FOR CHANGE

Students can be taught the important use of petitions to a responsible authority to ask for an action or to demonstrate public sentiment. Petitions enable persons who won't write personal letters to express their views at a public hearing to show a group consensus. When the more active members of a community spearhead such action, the list of names grows quickly. This is an easy, effective way to voice public opinion about concerns. Students can begin by selecting an "earthkeeping" proposal for student support.

The wording of the petition must be clear and the purpose of the statement or request carefully thought out. (If some of the signatures are those of community leaders, you will create a greater impact with this vehicle of group expression.)

A classroom teacher can enlist the aid of parents to take students to meetings of environmentally concerned groups in order to obtain current information and learn action possibilities. Students should be advised to listen and read before making up their minds on which side they wish to be counted. The teacher should constantly guide students to think and to form opinions based on information and research. How students support and express their opinions can make the difference in achieving constructive action on their favorite ecology project.

How to Prepare a Petition

1. State the purpose of the petition and to whom it is addressed. Word it with short statements and simple language. Support the purpose in a few paragraphs.
2. Allow spaces for names, addresses and phone numbers (optional) of signers.
3. Reproduce copies to distribute to local groups and for placement in business establishments. People on busy street corners can also be urged to sign the petition.
4. Check to see if a city permit is needed to circulate the petition. If you are circulating a petition on school grounds, get permission from the administration.
5. Decide on a date when all petitions should be gathered and how they can be presented for greatest persuasive impact.

Volunteers who help with the circulation of a petition need to understand the issues and ramifications so that they can answer questions from persons they approach for signatures and support. A friendly and alert manner in talking with people is very important in gathering signatures. Avoid being argumentative. A classroom role playing session can help prepare students to be effective volunteers.

PLAN A COMPLETE CLASS PROJECT

Put a little action into the classroom by asking students to define a specific ecological project, task or issue on which they feel they can be effective alone or with helpers. Distribute this outline as a guide.

I. Investigate and research ecological concerns, issues and problems in your community.
   A. Poll class members to determine the ecological project they would like to support as a group.

   B. Chart a time schedule to reach goals, long range and short term.
   C. Ask adults in the community for their support in helping you carry through your project.
 II. Define your special project; organize a program.
   A. Write letters to local, state, or national organizations to gain information about pollution abatement.
   B. Collect newspaper, magazine and journal clippings related to your ecological concerns.
III. Publicize the project.
   A. Plan an advertising campaign of slogans, posters and news items for the school and community newspapers about your environmental concerns and special project.
   B. Attend meetings of community related groups working on ecological problems.
   C. Chart your daily conservation efforts on a classroom bulletin board.

GALVANIZING ENERGY INTO A SUPER PROJECT

Student planning for a reunion in 25 years to unearth a buried time capsule can be an exciting project introduced by an innovative social studies teacher. The teacher can initiate a Time Capsule Project to "rev up" student motivation and interest in history. The purpose of the time capsule is to preserve information about our daily life so that pupils in later years can make comparisons and view firsthand the making of history. This medium is excellent for dramatizing how information about life today becomes tomorrow's history.

To initiate the project, an archeologist can be invited to discuss digs in other lands, what archeologists look for and where they find it. Ancient artifacts can provide fascinating topics for exploration. (The opportunity for exploring career possibilities in the field of archeology and history can also be correlated with such a project.)

Based on that information, students can plan the kinds of "artifacts" that would reflect their civilization. In the buried capsule they may include: A world map, pictures and models of current cars, buses, planes, bicycles, motorcycles and airplanes; newspaper clippings of supermarket advertisements, radio and television logs, photographs showing fashions of today in clothing and hairstyles; architectural designs of homes and public buildings; news accounts of sports events, space travel, body transplants, etc. Where appropriate, prices and costs should be included.

News accounts and commentaries on current problems such as food shortages, drug abuse, pollution, the energy crisis, crime, overpopulation, abandonment of personal property, Watergate and President Nixon's resignation will make interesting historical reading at the turn of the next century. So will taped samples of popular music, textbooks, telephone and city directories, employment contracts and salary scales.

Perhaps the capsule could be made of concrete lined in asphalt by a local vault company and donated to the school. The burial place would be marked and directions left with the school for unearthing 25 years from the day of its burial. Members of the class might videotape the burial of the time capsule. Part of the uncarthing ceremony would then include a view of how people looked in the 1970's.

9

Building Independence and Responsibility

Every human being has the power to be a productive person—producing goods, services, ideas or feelings that are helpful and valuable to others. Sometimes, though, we set up barriers to our own success. We perpetuate attitudes and expressions that impede positive relationships; we repeat behavior that is non-productive and reinforces our sense of failure.

To help students break down personal barriers to success, the teacher can create activities that help youngsters recognize their feelings and how they interact with others, what they do that works for them, and how they can change negative behavior patterns into more positive ones.

Dealing realistically with one's strengths and one's limitations is essential to any effort to improve oneself. Recognizing the possibility of change is basic to assuming responsibility for accomplishing change. The activities in this chapter focus on self-discovery and potentialities for change that are within reach of those with the courage to risk the status quo. The sensitive teacher can serve as an accepting and supportive guide, helping students select and achieve reasonable and workable goals for personal as well as academic development.

EXPANDING SELF-AWARENESS

Self-awareness is understanding how and why we do the things we do and how we react to people and situations. Rhythms and patterns are evident in our lives. Day and night break into patterns, seasons change; we sleep, work and play. We also develop patterns in how we talk to people, how we respond to requests, how we think and how we deal with responsibilities. We need to be aware of them. Do we feel comfortable with these patterns and do they help us meet our goals, or do we need to consider a change of behavior?

Some teens are so unsure of themselves that they are like blurred images projected on a screen. They need to bring the indefinite and diffused ideas about themselves into better focus. A teacher can help students focus on these questions and center on patterns and habits that need modifying.

An activity to build students' awareness of motives that determine personal behavior can begin with the filmstrip "Why Am I Afraid to Tell You Who I Am?"[1] The teacher can facilitate discussion by asking students to reflect on the roles that people play in the filmstrip, how they assert themselves, how they manipulate people, and how they are manipulated.

The filmstrip is supplemented by a book which is also called *Why Am I Afraid to Tell You Who I Am?* and by character cards. The cards show personality caricature and can be used in many ways. There are 40 cards labeled with titles such as "The Martyr," "The Pouter," "The Flirt." Students can examine the cards and talk about the personalities that are caricatured, and then take part in role playing. The cartoon style of the format is appealing to teens.

HELPING STUDENTS ZERO-IN ON THEMSELVES: SELF-EVALUATION ACTIVITIES

Start with a positive outlook. Teachers can assist students to realistically assess themselves and to build strategies which rein-

---

[1] "Why Am I Afraid to Tell You Who I Am?" (Niles, Illinois: Argus Communications, Department K, 1972).

force positive concepts about their attributes. Let the unit begin as each student focuses on his or her special qualities. Stress that each individual is a special person who has special talents.

Have students work with their friends to complete the self-quiz and personality profile that appear here as Figures 1 and 2.

As a follow-up activity, ask each student to divide a sheet of paper into three columns. In the first, the student is to list skills he has in getting along with agemates; in the second, interpersonal skills he would like to develop; in the third, the steps he could take to reach his goals for improving himself.

Figure 1: Self Quiz—
Zero in on the Real You!

Questions

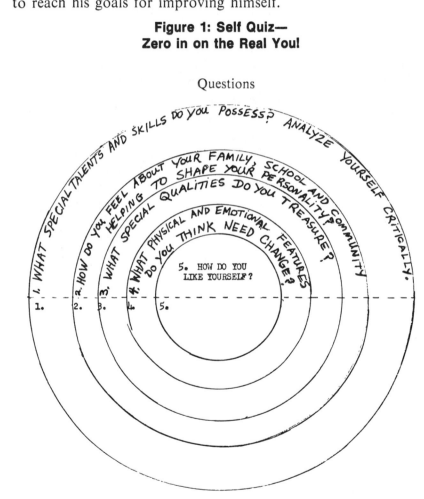

Write your answers below the dotted line.

Figure 2: Chart Your Own Personalty Profile

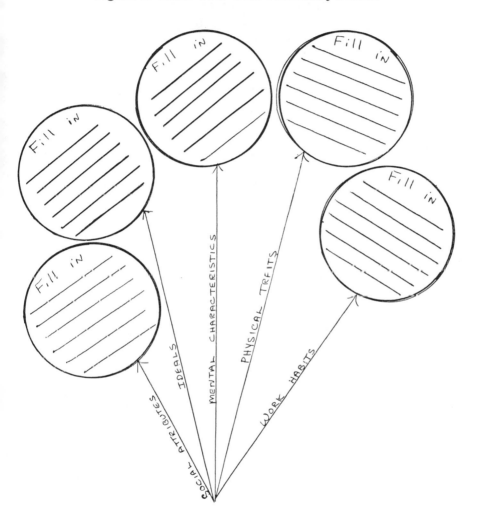

A SCRAPBOOK ON ME!

A scrapbook on oneself can be an excellent tool for self-assessment and provide a vehicle for examining how others see us.

Students are to include in their scrapbooks information about their physical traits, work habits, mental characteristics, social attributes, moral convictions, fun activities, ideals. Have them include examples, where possible, such as of times they used self-control even though circumstances were difficult and temptations were great. In this scrapbook, ask them to set out a section with photos of their family and special friends, their hobbies, and places they have visited.

WHO AM I?

For enrichment, ask students to select from magazines and newspapers pictures of activities, things, and people that they like and then create a collage of these pictures. They may then exchange these collages within the classroom. Have other students analyze the collage and write a profile of the person who submitted it. Knowledge of special interests will be gleaned as well as self-knowledge, as each student analyzes how another person sees himself in relation to people and things around him.

WHAT CAN I DO?

Self-confidence—the willingness to rely on one's own resources for making important decisions, the conviction that one can ultimately reach one's goals—must be based on a realistic self assessment, not just on optimism. A checklist such as the one that follows can help the teacher determine important directions for improvement, and can indicate to youngsters where more effort may be needed.

Yes	No	(Check one):
—	—	1. Can I perform well in at least one skill?
—	—	2. Can I gain personal satisfaction from developing this skill?
—	—	3. Can I apply skills learned at school to a job of my choice?

Yes	No	(Check one):
—	—	4. Can I perform well on this job because I have the necessary intelligence and aptitudes?
—	—	5. Can I be objective when I analyze my capabilities and strengths and not belittle myself because of previous defeats?
—	—	6. Can I pursue my goals securely because of the skills I have and the ability I have to improve?

WHAT CAN I BE?

Another self-study lesson might begin with these instructions:

Study yourself and make an analysis of habits you now possess. Decide which of these should be kept, which should be augmented or developed further, and which should be scrapped. Start with the question, "What kind of person do I want to become?" This picture will give you clues to the new habits you may want to develop.

WHAT WOULD I DO?

Have students consider the many possible responses to the same set of circumstances. Probe the use of rewards, restrictions, threats, compromise, manipulation, power struggles, and confrontation as means of solving problems. Discuss a hypothetical situation in which two people from differing backgrounds are faced with the same circumstances. Consider how their approaches to solution might differ.

Help students take a closer look at themselves with these activities.

- Make a balance sheet of past relationships with friends. Ask students to retrace friendships which have been successful, then analyze how they functioned to achieve satisfaction in these relationships.
- Assign each student to keep a log of how he feels each day for two weeks. Does he have more happy days than unhappy ones? Is he satisfied or dissatisfied with his attainments?
- Encourage students to keep a timetable of how each day's hours are spent. The student's record of how his time is spent will help

him determine his daily patterns. What kinds of people and actions bug him? What does he like to do? Are the telephone, television and sports activities sapping the energies needed for school
assignments? Hopefully, he will decide to make changes where
needed to include other activities and persons so that the positive
days outweigh the negative.

● Introduce crisis situations and ask students to respond to them.
Grade students on how they managed the crisis. Can they be
decisive in each situation and yet sensitive to others?

Reinforcing productive actions and good decision making in
students encourages them to be actively involved in their own
destinies.

THE TRICK BAG

The trick bag is middle-western jargon for a self-deluding
trap into which a person can fall. The trick bag is full of games
that people play. Just as in *Alice in Wonderland,* things are not
always as they seem.

A student doesn't have to be a magician to come out of his
trick bag. All he needs is to focus on how he deludes himself.
However, this can be an overwhelming task when faced alone. A
teacher can help students get in touch with their motives and the
games they play while engaging them in transactional discussions
and getting tasks done each day in the classroom.

For example, young women may fall into the trick bag of
seeking traditionally feminine roles such as secretary or nurse, instead of seeking out other interesting jobs or learning a trade. This
is because they have been conditioned to "stay in their place" and
feel out of place in sections of the job market that have been
labeled a man's. Girls often trick themselves and allow others to
trick them into treating male/female myths as truths.

> . . . the girl, since childhood, and whether she intends to stay
> within or go beyond the bounds of femininity, has looked to
> the male for fulfillment and escape; he wears the shining face
> of Perseus or St. George; he is the liberator, he is rich and
> powerful, he holds the keys to happiness.[2]

---

[2]Simone de Beauvior, "The Formative Years: The Young Girl," *The Second
Sex* (New York: Modern Library 1968), p. 328. Reprinted with the permission of
the publisher, Alfred A. Knopf, Inc.

Adolescents try out many roles which are incompatible with their real selves. As they reach maturity, they adapt, discard, and integrate others into their new adult roles. Teens need to know that when their actions meet disapproval, it is because of what they *do* and not what they *are*.

"I'M OKAY, YOU'RE OKAY"

"I'm okay; you're okay"[3] is Dr. Thomas Harris' statement of a healthy life position. The basic assumption is that we can get along with others if we feel we are okay and healthy in our approach to others and they, in turn, can communicate and get along with us.

Perceptions of how different temperament is revealed in interpersonal relationships can be useful to teens who are in a quandary about how their behavior is perceived by others. Behavior is purposeful and sometimes teens mimic behavior that they feel is liked by other teens only to find that they are perceived differently when they mimic others.

A positive mental attitude, a desire to communicate in a productive, healthy way can be the first step in conquering barriers to success. The human mind has infinite variety and expressive powers. The greater one's ability to bounce back after refusal or rejection or failure, the better are the chances of achieving one's goals—socially and in a career.

GAME CONTROL

Patterns of social interaction have been referrred to as "games people play."[4] To build an awareness of unhealthy game playing, a teacher can introduce this quiz to clarify game strategy that is used between people in school.

From the list which follows can you identify three games you play?

Can you identify three games you have seen others play?

What is your goal in playing these games?

What do you think is the goal of others' playing games?

---

[3]Thomas D. Harris, *I'm Okay: You're Okay* (New York: Harper & Row, 1967).

[4]Eric Berne, *Games People Play: The Psychology of Human Relationships* (New York: Grove Press, 1964).

Games People Play

"How far can I go in disrupting the class without getting sent out of the room?"

"The teacher calls on me infrequently to answer questions because I have conned her into thinking I am stupid."

"Someone is always getting me in trouble and the teacher blames me."

"How can I bug my parents today?"

"Feigning illness is a way to get out of work."

"I call attractive classmates on the telephone pretending I need the homework assignment."

As with sex-role stereotyping, name calling is a game that people play. Labeling people may be convenient but it can be detrimental too. The connotation of words used to describe personality can be explored in an English or social studies class. Discuss these words and the personality characteristics that are conjured up by each of them. How are these words alike and how are they different?

- Cooperative, saintly, a goody-two-shoes, a pollyanna
- Dependent, lazy, stupid, a follower
- Funny, silly, a character, a wise guy
- Aggressive, take charge, a know-it-all, devious
- Clever, foxy, a con-man, creative
- Emotional, defensive, a weakling, cry-baby

SOCIAL INTERACTION

In small group discussions, students can participate in transactions among themselves while building interpersonal communications skills. Skills in the process of problem solving can be learned as students focus on identifying a problem, making specific observations, listening to others, drawing conclusions, and expressing their own opinions. Since the discussions are student-directed, this is also a good way to build class morale.

A teacher can serve as a group leader helping students to build self-awareness, but preaching and reacting critically to students' comments is to be avoided at all costs. Over-directing also tends to stifle open discussion.

Group guidelines are helpful before classroom discussions get underway. The focus in these guidelines should be on productive discussion, staying on the subject and avoiding humiliating others. Rules for participation in the group should be developed by the students to protect the rights of all participants. Those who monopolize a discussion and those who need to be drawn into the discussion should be observed closely and individually guided.

OPENING A DIALOGUE

The teacher can begin the group interaction process by presenting a problem that might affect a teen. Then, through discussion, students can analyze the kind of person who might have this problem and how he might resolve it. Problems such as controlling anger, expressing feelings, reacting to criticism, can be focal points. Guide students in answering questions such as these on anger:

- Identify a situation when you got angry. What was the reason behind your feeling of anger?
- What did you say? What do you *wish* you had said or done? Toward whom was your anger directed?
- How did you overcome the angry feelings?
- What kinds of interactions make you angry?
- How might you change the way you react to anger?

Students can be helped to realize that feelings must be recognized and accepted before they can be dealt with. Anger, for example, can be inappropriate and counter-productive in some situations. In others, it can be an indicator of strength of convictions.

A social studies teacher can begin classroom discussion by talking about predicaments which caused some world-renowned persons to slip into controversy or conflict. Encourage students to research information on personalities such as General MacArthur, the Beatles, Jim Thorpe, President Nixon, President Truman, Frances Baker Eddy, Margaret Sanger, Cesar Chavez, Malcolm X, Khrushchev. Unfolding the personality of well-known people can be eye opening to students who feel programmed for failure. They find that even the best-loved and most respected persons have made errors in judgment.

PINPOINTING PROBLEMS THROUGH SMALL GROUP DISCUSSION

Small group discussions on subjects such as the following can initiate healthy interaction among students:

- How I get into trouble.
- What bugs me about kids my age.
- Communicating with parents and teachers isn't easy.
- Loneliness causes me to feel unhappy.
- Love is a serious matter.
- How I cope with fear.
- How I persuade people to do things my way.

Also, quotations that reveal attitudes and personalities can be discussed. For example, in *Our Foreign Born Citizens*,[5] Spyros Skouras, a movie theatre magnate, is quoted as saying: "No mariner ever distinguished himself on a smooth sea." What does this statement tell us about the speaker and how he faced adversity?

From *The Best and the Brightest*,[6] a statement about Walter Rostow: "He had the great capacity not to see what he did not choose to see," can be examined and analyzed in the context of everyday life.

In the process of discussing how people reveal their attitudes, the disruptive student and the un-motivated student can join their classmates in centering on public personalities instead of on themselves as culprits and targets of attention. Besides quotes from non-fiction, students can select statements from newspapers, magazines, and fiction. The class discussion can then be focused on observable characteristics, verbal and non-verbal, that are considered favorable or unfavorable.

AVOIDING NON-PRODUCTIVE BEHAVIOR

Choices and chances to grasp new opportunities can mean crisis decisions for students. The great tragedy is that frequently they do not know how to accomplish their goals in productive,

---

[5]Annie Beard, *Our Foreign Born Citizens,* 6th ed. (New York: Thomas Y. Crowell, 1968), p. 210.

[6]David Halberstam. *The Best and the Brightest* (New York: Random House, 1972) p. 637.

self-realizing ways. Sometimes they are too dependent on others. Sometimes they want the promise of the television advertisement: "We guarantee these results if you make this decision."

There are no guarantees in life but, with systematic planning, students can learn to realize some of their dreams and hopes. How can we take crises and turn them into attitudinal commitments that will be helpful and healthful? Knowledge is the first step and the teacher can certainly help.

Each person has attitudes, values, feelings which determine his behavior. Behavior is purposeful but sometimes teens are unaware of the purpose and, therefore, experience dissonance in their lives.

Some teens are convinced that they cannot achieve the goals they desire. However, many times they never wanted those goals in the first place. Or, they may find, satisfying one need interferes with satisfying another. With recognition, these conflicts may be resolved.

When we begin to focus on conflicts and weaknesses we may feel troubled and uneasy. We may not like what we see. The teacher can reinforce the idea that everyone experiences anxiety in facing the new and unknown. Questioning one's habits of thinking is not easy. The challenge of self-understanding brings self-doubts, but with sensitivity and careful planning, doubt can become a motivating factor for change.

As the teacher assists students in learning about themselves she can help them to modify behavior patterns that impede their achieving personal goals and contributing to society. As students critically analyze themselves, perhaps the teacher can help some of them to recognize the defenses that lead them into unacceptable behavior.

For example, a student may derive temporary gratification from the feeling that non-conformity makes him appear superior and strong. Why does the student compete in an unproductive way to gain attention in the class? Does he have a personal goal to reach in his peer culture?

Behavior such as talking disruptively, forgetting books and supplies, interrupting other students as they work, name calling during classroom discussions, irregular attendance, can be discussed on a one-to-one basis with the student in order to find alternative, acceptable modes of behavior. Then, just as team strategy works in sports, class members can join in discussion and develop supportive techniques to help each other bring about changes. (See Chapter 10 for specific ways to initiate change patterns.)

Books about social problems can help to focus discussion on non-productive forms of behavior and enable youngsters to see the positive alternatives that are available to them. While some teachers may encounter school limitations on classroom subject matter, an effort should be made to foster candid and free-wheeling discussion of topics which students will find meaningful.

Mention possible topics for students to explore, topics such as those that follow. Divide the class into small groups, allowing students to choose their preferred topics. Have each group make a class presentation of the materials they explored while investigating their topic. Encourage full class discussion of each topic.

Group 1: Gang Affiliations

The urban ghetto student makes use of survival skills which he learns early in his home and street experiences. Such a student frequently finds status and protection in a street gang. (His membership may be an important identification for him but very little mastery of academic skills will be achieved in that framework.)

Establishing a Dialogue

The innovative teacher might use the street experiences of these students to establish a dialogue with them. With careful planning you can also use the experiences of others to motivate desirable attitudes for solving problems and disciplining oneself.

For example, after reading a description of a teen-age gang war, the teacher can spark interest in the topic by asking these questions:

1. What is your reaction to teen-age gangs? Do you belong? Do you want to belong?
2. Have you ever been asked to join a gang? Why or why not?
3. Have you ever been threatened for not joining?
4. Did your older brothers or sisters belong?
5. What are the advantages and disadvantages of membership?

This topic should arouse instant interest among boys in the classroom, since they are the ones who are principally affected by teen-age gang membership. Parallels can be drawn to many types of group membership, however.

Have a student read aloud a series of jackets from books about gang activities to interest his or her classmates in reading these books:

Suggested Readings on Gang Affiliations

Fact

Cervantes, Lucius F. *The Drop-out; Causes and Cures.* Ann Arbor, Michigan: University of Michigan Press, 1965.

Fry, John R. *Fire and Blackstone.* Philadelphia: Lippincott, 1969.

Mayerson, Charlotte L. *Two Blocks Apart.* New York: Holt, Rinehart & Winston, 1965.

Fiction

Beim, Jerrold. *Trouble After School.* New York: Harcourt, Brace & World, 1967.

Bonham, Frank. *Durango Street.* New York: Dutton, 1965.

Carson, John F. *The Twenty-Third Street Crusaders.* New York: Farrar, Straus & Giroux, 1958.

Friedman, Frieda. *Ellen and the Gang.* New York: William Morrow, 1963.

Group 2: Runaways

In discontent and rebellion, teens sometimes turn in directions that are difficult for adults to understand—toward the bewildering world of drugs, toward a peer culture or toward the birth of a new culture.

William Pennell Rock coined a phrase the "Great American Rebellation" when he expressed his fear and awe that teens' revelations may be consequent upon rebellion against the law and that their rebellion may be consequent on alternative ways of being human but nonetheless revelations.[7]

---

[7]William Pennell Rock, "Alienation: Yes, Patriotism: Yes," *The Center Magazine,* IV (November-December, 1971), p. 7.

William Rock is indicating an alienation that many young people in our society feel. They reject "the system" that seems to be the cause of so many personal problems and seek alternative life styles. This is one way of demonstrating the independence they feel.

A teacher can steer class discussion to illustrate how compromise is often helpful in decision-making, and that a complete abandonment of adult suggestions is often unwise.

Suggest that students interview their friends about this topic. First, design a questionnaire. Here is a sample that might be usable by the group studying this topic:

1. Have you ever felt like running away from home?
2. What caused you to feel this way?
3. How did you resolve this problem?
4. Did you actually run away?
5. Where did you go? Where were you planning to go?
6. Does running away cause problems or create answers? Explain your reply.

Let the group select a chairperson. The chairperson will tabulate the answers and report on the results to the class. Encourage students to read fiction dealing with this topic and analyze how realistic it is.

Suggested Readings on Run Aways

Fact

Dorman, Michael. *Under 21.* New York: Delacorte Press, 1970.

Horwitz, Elinor L. *Communes in America; the Place Just Right.* Philadelphia: Lippincott, 1972.

Jr. Scholastic magazine. December 6, 1973 issue.

Time, Inc. *The Hippies.* Ed. by Joe David Brown. New York: Time, Inc., 1967.

Fiction

Colman, Hila. *Claudia, Where Are You?* New York: Morrow, 1969.

Cone, Molly. *You Can't Make Me If I Don't Want To.* Boston: Houghton Mifflin Co., 1971.

Crane, Caroline. *Stranger on the Road.* New York: Random House, 1971.

Heffron, Dorris. *A Nice Fire and Some Moonpennies.* New York: Atheneum, 1972.

Fiction

Kingman, Lee. *The Peter Pan Bag.* Boston: Houghton Mifflin Co., 1970.

Robinson, Joan G. *Charley.* New York: Coward, McCann and Geoghegan, 1970.

Group 3: Drug Abuse

A pill, a joint, a drink, a hypodermic needle—the desire to try something new because everybody else is—or at least those from whom teenagers seek acceptance—can lead to tragedy. Pain, confusion, sensory excitement, euphoria, depression, and guilt are some of the results of chemical abuse. Books about such experiences may emphasize the ineffectiveness of mood-changing chemicals as problem solvers.

To activate students to participate in classroom activities, a teacher may encourage the adaptation of the dialogue in some novels to radio scripts or plays. Ask students to select the dialogue and perhaps to ad-lib. Tape the sessions and dub in appropriate music. The book, *Escape From Nowhere*,[8] which deals with drug experimentation, lends itself to this approach. Other books on this topic follow:

Suggested Readings on Drug Abuse

Fact	Fiction
Berry, James. *Heroin Was My Best Friend.* New York: Crowell-Collier, 1971.	Bonham, Frank. *Cool Cat.* New York: E.P. Dutton, 1971.
Brenner, Joseph H., *et al. Drugs and Youth; Medical Psychiatric and Legal Facts.* New York: Liveright, 1970.	Chaber, M.E. *The Acid Nightmare.* New York: Holt, Rinehart & Winston, 1967.
De Bold, Richard C. and Russell C. Leaf, editors.	Coles, Robert. *The Grass Pipe.* Boston: Little, Brown and Co., 1969.

---

[8]Jeannette Eyerly, *Escape From Nowhere* (Philadelphia: Lippincott, 1969).

Fact	**Fiction**

Fact

LSD, Man and Society. Middleton, Conn.: Wesleyan University Press, 1967.

Dorman, Michael. *Under 21.* New York: Delacorte Press, 1970.

Gersh, Marvin and Iris Litt. *The Handbook of Adolescence.* New York: Stein and Day, 1971.

Gorodetzky, Charles W. and Samuel T. Christian. *What You Should Know About Drugs.* New York: Harcourt Brace Jovanovich, 1970.

Houser, Norman W. *Drugs; Facts on Their Use and Abuse.* New York: Lothrop, Lee and Shepard, 1969.

Hyde, Margaret O., ed. *Mind Drugs.* New York: McGraw-Hill, 1968.

Lieberman, Mark. *The Dope Book; All About Drugs.* New York: Praeger Publishers, 1972.

Madison, Arnold. *Drugs and You.* New York: Julian Messner, 1972.

Rosevear, John. *Pot; A Handbook of Marijuana.* New York: University Books, 1967.

Vermes, Hal and Jean Vermes. *Helping Youth Avoid 4 Great Dangers: Smoking,*

Fiction

Emery, Anne. *The Sky is Falling.* Philadelphia: Westminster Press, 1970.

Eyerly, Jeannette. *Escape From Nowhere.* Philadelphia: Lippincott, 1969.

Kerr, M.E. *Dinky Hocker Shoots Smack.* New York: Harper, 1972.

Walden, Amelia Elizabeth. *Same Scene, Different Place.* Philadelphia: Lippincott, 1969.

Fact

Drinking, VD, Narcotics Addiction. New York: Association Press, 1965.

Readers may also obtain up-to-date information from the National Clearinghouse for Drug Abuse Information, 5454 Wisconsin Avenue, Chevy Chase, Maryland 20015.

Group 4: Alcoholism

One of the most tragic family problems is that which is created by alcoholism. Alcoholism not only affects adults, but many teen-agers as well. Destroyer of mind and body, alcohol has become a serious problem for those who start this destructive habit early in their lives.

Invite a panel from Alcoholic Anonymous or Alanon to speak to the class to culminate a reading assignment on the following titles:

Suggested Readings on Alcoholism

Fact

Block, Marvin A. *Alcoholism; Its Facets and Phases.* Boston: Day, 1965.

Dorman, Michael. *Under 21.* New York: Delacorte, 1970.

Hornick, Edith. *You and Your Alcoholic Parent.* New York: Association Press, 1974.

Plaut, Thomas F.A. *Alcohol Problems;* A Report to the Nation by the Cooperative Commis-

Fiction

Colman, Hila. *Car-Crazy Girl.* New York: William Morrow, 1967.

Ellis, Ella. *Celebrate the Morning.* New York: Atheneum, 1972.

Johnson, Annabel and Edgar Johnson. *Count Me Gone.* New York: Simon and Schuster, 1968.

Summers, James L. *The Long Ride Home.* Philadelphia: Westminster Press, 1968.

Fact	Fiction
sion on the Study of Alcoholism. Oxford University Press, 1967. Vermes, Hal and Jean Vermes. *Helping Youth Avoid 4 Great Dangers: Smoking, Drinking, VD, Narcotics Addiction.* New York: Association Press, 1965.	Woody, Regina. *One Day at a Time.* Philadelphia: Westminster Press, 1968.

Seeking causes and reasons, interpreting and explaining are ways of understanding experience and resolving problems. To help students get in touch with fictional experiences, ask them to look for the answers to these questions:

1. How did the characters in the novel feel?
2. What were they experiencing?
3. What did they feel physically?
4. Did the experience cause them mental anguish?
5. Did the experience make them feel happy?
6. How did their actions affect others?

This group may also want to prepare a panel discussion based on the material explored about alcoholism. You might suggest a discussion of the similarities and differences between alcohol abuse and drug abuse. Encourage class members to ask questions of those who researched the topics.

BUILDING INDEPENDENCE AND RESPONSIBILITY

There are many factors that explain why a person behaves as he does. Some factors are innate, others are learned. Some are responses to a particular set of environmental circumstances. Some are the result of the influence of other people.

We are all subject to the influences of others. But accepting that influence does not imply relinquishing our independence or autonomy. Rather, as we mature, we learn to sort out the advice and direction we receive, select that which is helpful and appropriate to our needs, and reject the rest. In the process, we learn more about ourselves, we improve the way we handle difficult situations, and we assume more and more responsibility for our own behavior.

Taking Criticism

Because of the uncertainty that most teenagers feel about themselves, criticism and advice may be hard to accept. Help students become more aware of themselves and their responses to criticism by discussing recent situations in which they have been the recipient of the advice of a teacher, parent or counselor. Ask students, for example:

What were the circumstances under which the advice was given?
How did you feel upon hearing it?
How did you react?
Has it proven to be appropriate or helpful?

Ask students to recall situations when their parents gave them advice. Does parental advice contain many do's and don'ts? Why is this? How do they react to parental advice? Do they tend to give advice to others or only to listen to it?

ASSERTIVENESS TRAINING

If adults insist upon telling youngsters what to do and what not to do, we deprive them of opportunities to experience their own competence, to assert themselves for a positive purpose, to succeed and to fail—and to practice the kinds of behavior that make the difference. Classroom experiences can be based on their own backgrounds, on the lives of others, or on the analysis of direct classroom activities.

Assertiveness training can begin by story telling to encourage students' modeling real life figures. Story telling does not have to be limited to elementary grade students. Turning to the book, *Who Says You Can't?*[9] a teacher can find good examples of individuals who bucked the establishment to achieve social reform.

Each week you might tell the story of one of the persons discussed in *Who Says You Can't?*

A. Ralph Nader, the consumer lobbyist.
B. Gene Wirges, a newspaperman who bucked a political machine.
C. Leon Sullivan, a campaigner for economic equality at a job-training center.

---

[9]Beryl and Samuel Epstein, *Who Says You Can't?* (New York: Coward-McCann, Inc., 1969).

    D. Frances Kelsey and Helen Taussig, scientists whose insights into the effects of the drug thalidomide prevented untold infant deformities.

    E. Joseph Papp, initiator of popular free theatre in New York City.

Additional Activities

Debating is a form of an educational game in which students can interact directly and display problem-solving skills as they take sides to debate different topics.

Debating teams might be designed as:

Teams		Sample Topics
1. Serfs	Nobleman	Any nobleman should have the power to subject any serf to his will.
2. Plantation Owners	Slaves	Had it not been for the goodness of plantation owners, most of the slaves would have died in the new country.
3. Children	Parents	The "generation gap" is in part caused by the "communication gap" between children and parents.
4. Teachers	Students	Were it not for the indifference of some teachers, there would be no dropouts.
5. Salespersons	Customers	Customers are *not* always right; and salespersons should *not* have to withstand their insults.
6. Army Privates	Sergeants	(Add on)
7. Employers	Union Members	
8. Business Executives	Lawmakers	
9. Defendants	Judges	

Each class selects a referee. Students may score the debate by evaluating which side was most effective in arguing a point of view. Two goals are to improve class attention span and to encourage thinking through lessons and understanding historical theories and events.

ANALYZING LEADERSHIP AND RESPONSIBILITY

To steer students away from fatalistic ideas about their destinies and to encourage them to stake out their own future means building their awareness of their leadership abilities. Tracing the factors in the personality development of well known persons can awaken students to the turning points that may lead to their own success in leadership roles.

Books that contain short selections on contemporary, well known persons will hold the interest of the students who can analyze how each person's life developed. Also, students will visualize how much they have in common with persons who have succeeded in building a successful life for themselves.

When I was Sixteen[10] contains high interest interviews with eighteen outstanding women from such varying backgrounds as Lady Bird Johnson, wife of the late president; Marisa Berenson, a talented model; Margaret Mead, outstanding anthropologist. Their lives are highly diverse, yet their reflections about their experiences offer a perspective to the reader on changes that everyone goes through. An emphasis on factors which are selected by us and those that are foisted on us can be mind openers for those who are inclined to cry, "It's not my fault," to everything adverse that happens to them.

History can attest to eminent men and women who did not achieve well during certain periods of their school careers. Another activity can introduce persons such as the great mathematician Albert Einstein, former presidents Franklin D. Roosevelt and John F. Kennedy, and Sir Winston Churchill as persons who also faced troublesome days in their school careers. A study of their lives can be instrumental in setting the tone for change and hope.

------

[10] Mary Brannum, et al., *When I Was Sixteen* (New York: Platt and Munk, 1967).

Motivation is an aspect of personality that can be triggered in different ways. Sometimes acquiring a special interest in a topic can create strong motivation. For example, Wernher von Braun, a famous space scientist, failed high school courses in math and physics.[11] However, as his interest in rocketry developed, he began excelling in math and physics.

Government leaders offer still another approach to analyzing qualities of leadership. Our interest, our activities, our loves— these constitute our real selves. Adding up the plusses and minuses of leadership traits observed and studied in political figures can be a way of pinpointing the curious amalgam of public interest and self-interest that is reflected in government leaders.

The qualities of leadership exemplified in some of these leaders can be analyzed from quoted excerpts from David Halberstam's *The Best and the Brightest*.[12]

> Bob McNamara was a remarkable man in a remarkable era. He would, for instance, lie, dissemble, not just to the public; they all did that in varying degrees, but inside, in high-level meetings always for the good of the cause, always for the right reason, always to serve the office of the President.[13]

Discussing Robert Kennedy at a briefing about Vietnam, Halberstam reveals the responses Kennedy received when he asked top members of the mission: "Do you have any problems?" "No" said everyone in unison; there were no problems. Then he asked if anyone wanted to speak to him in private about problems. They all did. Thus he learned a lesson about what people would say for the record and what they would say in private.[14]

Of Lyndon Johnson, Halberstam wrote:

> He was a man with an extraordinary attention to detail which was very important to him; larger conceptions might not mean that much, but if he knew the details he could control the action, he could control subordinates. So he

---

[11] E. Paul Torrance, "Motivating Children with Social Problems" in E. Paul Torrence and Robert D. Strom, eds., *Mental Health and Achievement* (New York: John Wiley & Sons, Inc., 1965), p. 339.

[12] David Halberstam, *The Best and the Brightest* (New York: Random House, 1972). Reprinted with the permission of the publisher, Random House, Inc.

[13] *Ibid.,* p. 219.

[14] *Ibid.,* p. 274.

always knew details about everyone, more about them than they knew of him.[15]

Discussion centering on leadership traits such as initiative, perseverance, and reliability can be useful in stressing the importance of personality and temperament in getting and keeping a job and in finding personal satisfaction in life. The following questions can be applied to any political figure discussed:

Questions for Discussion

1. What do the reflections say about the person?
2. What type of criticism does he face?
3. Does he seek changes?
4. How does he get cooperation?
5. What are his priorities and self-interests?
6. What interests lie in loyalties in society, humanity, nature, God?
7. What special contribution did the leader make?
8. How did each person react at a crucial decision-making time? (Use magazine and newspaper reports.)
9. Do you now, or have you in the past, felt free to disagree with decisions made by your parents, teachers, and other significant adults in your life?
10. Do you feel your opinions are seriously considered by classmates, teachers, and parents?
11. Thinking of yourself, would you say that some day you will make an important contribution to the welfare of the community or at least be active in the community? Explain your answer.

10

Classroom Control and Behavior Modification

On many mornings, a teacher may look out onto a roomful of fidgety, unmotivated students. In some cases, if the teaching process is to go on at all, the teacher must first address herself to controlling and disciplining disruptive youngsters. It is here that self-analysis and examination of causes need to be considered.

Grambs and others[1] offer the following circumstances as testing grounds for classroom control: the last five minutes before lunch; the last period of the day, especially Friday; the whole day before some special function such as a sporting event or a holiday; the period following an event such as a school assembly, fire drill or rally. The presence of a substitute teacher may signal to some students a chance to upset the class order.

Teachers may foster discipline problems by: employing the same teaching methods daily; having no lesson plan for the day; allowing filibustering to go on in the classroom; having no set rules or policies for classroom decorum; giving vague assignments; not following through on homework deadlines; not making students respect tardy bells; following a set curriculum,

---

[1] Jean D. Grambs *et al.*, *Modern Methods in Secondary Education*, rev. ed. (New York: Holt, Rinehart & Winston, Inc., 1958), p. 430. Reprinted with the permission of the publisher.

regardless of whether or not students comprehend the purposes for lessons and assignments; trying to out-shout students, rather than getting their attention before talking; not allowing for individual differences among students; "looking down" on students by bullying, ridiculing, belittling, or trying to incite fear.

GUIDELINES FOR CLASSROOM CONTROL

There is no set pattern for teachers to follow in handling classroom disturbances, but some suggestions may be helpful in attempting to establish classroom control.

Policies should be established and announced regarding classroom behavior such as hair care; chewing and popping gum; coming to class without pencils, paper or books; lying and cheating; arguing or fighting with other students or the teacher. Many loud disturbances may be intentionally provoked by the student who has mastered the art of inciting direct confrontation with the teacher in order to prevent the teaching process from continuing.

The teacher need not be a dictator, but youngsters should not be allowed to pressure him or her into doing or acting in compliance with their wishes. Within a democratic framework, both can become involved in setting acceptable standards for classroom behavior.

There is no need for teachers to accept chaos in the classroom. Seeing discipline needs in a newly organized way will enable us to transform our approach to problem solving, so that we enjoy success with greater frequency. We can avoid pitfalls that await those teachers who leave to chance and the diminishing momentum of past efforts the solving of classroom problems. That is our nemesis: repeating techniques that don't produce the results we want.

A scientific approach to classroom problems involves answering these questions:

What are we to do, or say?
Where will we do or say it?
When will we do or say it?
Who will do or say it?
Who is to be informed and when?
How will we know when we have arrived at our solution?

There will always be some discipline problems, but we can take steps to eliminate many and prevent more from arising. We can pinpoint them, outline the facts, and consider alternatives for their elimination.

Teachers sometimes need help in recognizing and dealing with stress-caused behavior in students and even in themselves. Continued stress has the effect of making one feel tense and unhappy. As teachers focus upon observable and quantifiable events, they can determine a systematic approach to problem detection and remediation. Since behavior problems are often made up of small acts, a workable approach to problem solving should encompass two elements: first, determination of a system for handling problems one step at a time; second, development of techniques for the measurement of degrees of change.

A SYSTEMS APPROACH TO SOLVING PROBLEMS

Developing a systematic approach to a behavior change process should include understanding the teacher's role, the counselor's role, and the student's role.

A good way to explain to the learner, the student, the conditions which he will be expected to meet is to write in simple terms certain objectives that you wish him to reach—when you wish him to reach them, what will be considered an acceptable level of performance, and how he might go about reaching these objectives.

Mager asks the key question, "What is the learner doing when he is demonstrating that he has achieved his objective?"[2] Mager instructs us to identify experiences in behavioristic language by (a) identifying the observable behavior or performance that will be accepted as evidence that the learner has achieved the objective, and (b) indicating time limits.

The teacher's first approach to solving a behavior problem is to identify in performance terms behavior to be changed; to identify conditions which elicit and maintain behavior; to review the consequences of behavior while determining whether or not a change is desired; to investigate and formulate alternative plans of action.

---

[2]Robert F. Mager, *Preparing Instructional Objectives* (Belmont, Calif.: Fearon Publishers, 1962), pp. 13-14.

The target behavior or performance that we wish to modify may be verbal or nonverbal. A behavioral objective specifies what the learner must be able to perform when he is demonstrating mastery of the objective. Mager indicates three parts of a well-formulated behavioral objective:

a. Behavior: What you are to perform or demonstrate.
b. Condition: Circumstances in which the behavior will be demonstrated.
c. Criterion: The acceptable level of performance at which the behavior must be demonstrated.[3]

We want to keep in mind the process of analyzing relationships, making predictions, evaluating consequences and taking actions relevant to educational, vocational and social goals. By formulating decisions and plans to improve our classrooms as learning places we can increase our stability and consistency in moving towards self-improvement goals and in helping others reach goals, too.

Let's break away from abstractions. Apathy and minimal effort are just two of the problems which are frequently mentioned by teachers. Indicating the range of conditions under which performance is expected is one thing; figuring out ways to teach or to reach that performance level is another task.

CREATING A CLIMATE FOR CHANGE

The basic elements for a mentally healthy climate are probably the same ones described by Carl Rogers in defining a constructive counseling relationship: empathy, congruence, and positive regard.[4]

A teacher reveals empathy when she is sensitive to her impact on the class and theirs on her. She gives encouragement and support to both disruptive and passive children, to help them expand their range of behavior.

The teacher indicates congruence when she consistently uses her authority and responsibility to communicate patterns of behavior which are in line with learning tasks and objectives.

---

[3]*Ibid.,* p. 12.
[4]Carl Rogers, *Client Centered Therapy* (New York: Houghton Mifflin, 1951).

Positive regard is revealed when the teacher does things that make the student feel accepted, worthwhile, that goals are within his reach, and that he compares well with others.

Let's define, design, and monitor the approaches we will use in modifying behavior, ours and that of our students. Information that can give us confidence that we know the kinds of work that will have to be done in order to progress toward the goal of eliminating classroom problems is a step toward self-improvement. The *telos* or end result of using these techniques can be personal growth in skill building and the termination of behavior that destroys the learning environment in a classroom.

BREAKING IN WITH BEHAVIOR MODIFICATION TECHNIQUES

Behavior modification is a process aimed at substituting appropriate behavior for inappropriate behavior. Its techniques are based on the principle of reinforcing positive acts as a way of encouraging their repetition. Behavior modification is most effective when it involves the subject in the process as a goal setter, an evaluator, and as a beneficiary of the rewards of change.

One strategy that has been used effectively in behavior modification is contingency contracting. A contingency contract is an agreement between two parties that states that "If you will do X, I will do Y." A student contract should state the performance objectives to be reached, a time period for accomplishment, how achievement will be measured and the rewards to be granted for satisfactory completion of the contract terms. An ongoing goal of contingency contracting is to teach students that their decisions have a direct impact on what happens in their lives.

Throughout this book, the problem of motivation has occupied a dominant position. As Hoover reminds us:

> One's teaching task in discipline is similar to his task in any other field. Children learn some things by listening, but they are more likely to remember and act on their *own words and ideas*...Youngsters will learn more quickly if they are permitted to assist in setting up their own rules of conduct.[5]

We're working at teaching students to become self-directed. Instead of the teacher appearing as a law-and-order agent of the

---

[5]Kenneth H. Hoover, *Learning and Teaching in the Secondary School*, 3rd ed. (Boston: Allyn and Bacon, 1972), p. 51.

school, the student must assume responsibility for motivating his own behavior. However, to provide the motivation for change we can offer concrete rewards attractive enough to encourage changes in behavior.

Motivation and discipline are components of the same problem. Indeed, when effective motivation is lacking, the problem of controlling and disciplining is chronic. However, by accepting motivation and discipline as equal aspects of the teaching process, the teacher can span the formidable hurdle of reaching and teaching the restless, mobile adolescent. In this context, the word *discipline* means teaching the art of restraining undesirable behavior and practicing desirable behavior both in their personal and social experiences.

Techniques for behavior modification are not magic stamps which, by some sort of voodoo power, can alleviate all classroom problems. There is no package deal to untangle all phases of unhealthy or disruptive classroom behavior. However, teachers can zero-in on three questions that may help to eliminate behavioral or communication problems in the classroom. First, the teacher might ask herself: What changes are desired? Second, what alternative strategies for change could be employed? Third, what alternatives appear to be the most effective and efficient?

Behavior modification techniques can work for you. Teachers can learn to spot clues which indicate stress or emotional pain and modify the situation before disruption leads to havoc. You can learn to see a problem early and prevent problems from persisting in the classroom.

The support of the administration of a school is necessary. Many times a principal will have the opportunity to refer a teacher to a counselor who can take the time to work out methods of problem solving. Case conferences can be a good place to zero-in on systematic problem solving. Also, if contingency contracting is to be fair to students, the principals need to be aware of what contracting means. Then the counselor and teacher can be assured of administrative support in their reward and reinforcement procedures.

A CASE STUDY

An eighth grade English teacher with ten years of teaching experience consulted with a school counselor regarding the difficulty she was having settling her class down to work after lunch every day. Also, many students were cutting the class. There didn't seem to be much change even after the principal visited the classroom.

The teacher indicated to the counselor: "I think these children have a host of problems. I especially would like you to help them find ways to ask questions and find answers without their resorting to 'acting-out.' This would serve a dual purpose, since more time could be spent drawing out those youngsters who have become increasingly withdrawn in such a noisy setting. Also, it would serve to help them to grow in their opinions of themselves and in their abilities, thereby enabling them to react more positively to each other."

The teacher described the behavior of one student in particular. Jane was guilty of frequently "acting out" in a disruptive way. Although she had leadership ability, Jane frequently reacted violently to criticism. One day she yelled "You are a bitch!" at the teacher. The other students seemed to enjoy goading her on. About every other week, Jane would be involved in a fight with someone in class. She rarely completed her assignments and her constant "blurting-out" (*i.e.*, talking out of turn or when not recognized or called on by the teacher) seemed to have an influence on other students who also began "blurting-out."

Studying the chaotic state of her classroom with the help of the counselor, the teacher was able to look objectively for ways to resolve the problem. In this case study, which will be illustrated intermittently throughout this chapter, the teacher began to eliminate the stressful situation in her classroom by first pinpointing the problem.

PINPOINTING PROBLEMS AND PROBLEM-SOLVING METHODS

Given a problem situation, the first step for the teacher to decide is what he or she wants to happen.

In the sample case, the teacher wanted Jane to complete assignments made in English class. She also wanted her to stop disrupting the class by "blurting-out," to recite when recognized, and not to be ready to fight at the least provocation or disagreement with other students or the teacher.

Next, the teacher should analyze conditions under which the change will take place.

When visiting the classroom the counselor noticed several environmental factors in addition to Jane's behavior. The teacher permitted students to sit where they liked. Several students were sitting at tables near the window. The conversation each day included talk about contemporary black militants and their justification in approaching problems by militant means. Not more than four of the same students were usually involved in these discussions.

The teacher spent an average of seven minutes each day reminding students to come to class on time and be seated promptly. Yet, when the tardy bell rang, the hallway outside the classroom was still full of her students. Several were just walking into the classroom. Students were allowed to bring soft drinks into the classroom and to chew gum.

Since environment has an effect on children's behavior, the teacher and counselor discussed possible modification of the classroom environment. The teacher agreed to assign seats. Students no longer had to hesitate and decide where to sit each day. Also the teacher no longer permitted soft drinks in the classroom. This change contributed to students' developing an on-the-job attitude in the class.

The teacher placed easy-to-answer questions related to class assignments on the blackboard for students to answer during the first five minutes of the hour. Those who answered the questions correctly were given bonus points toward their grade evaluation. These bonus questions served to focus students' attention on getting to class on time to gain bonus points.

Last, the teacher should analyze the extent or quality of the success at this point. We need to talk about concerns in terms which result in as complete and precise a description of the problem situation as possible. Using concrete and specific terms helps a teacher to pinpoint a problem and make it less overwhelming. Instead of beginning and ending with a statement like, "I am so frustrated," try to write down what you mean when you say you feel helpless. What are some of the times you feel that way? Now we are focusing on specific behavior and events and this helps us to understand a problem and then decide on ways to alleviate it.

Frequently, what the teacher does is not enough to bring about change. The student also needs to know what is expected of him so that change techniques can be implemented. Using the same methods of analysis, performance objectives can be defined by individual students and for the class.

PLANNING FOR CHANGE: A CHANGE FORMULA

Understanding a problem increases the probability of producing change. When the school counselor is asked to visit a classroom as a trained observer to help pinpoint stress factors and narrow the problem down to a level of understanding, several methods may be employed. The counselor can become a consultant to teachers, opening at least a two-way avenue of communication. And when parents become involved, a triangular dialogue will be established. The final essential element is the student himself. In addition to direct participation, information is needed on which to base the plan that will evolve.

To help plan the change process, the counselor in our case study of Jane interviewed her and provided the teacher with background information:

> The results of the Iowa Test of Basic Skills and the Lorge Thorndike Test of Mental Ability showed that Jane had the ability to perform at grade level. However, despite Jane's mental ability, she had received failing marks in English, math, and science, but had not been retained because of an "all pass" policy of the school.
>
> During a series of interviews with Jane, the counselor learned that Jane was the butt of her mother's violent temper when she was dissatisfied with Jane's chores at home. The older children in the family copied their mother's behavior and also shouted obsenities at Jane. She compensated by calling her female teachers "bitch" and by saying "shit" and "damn" whenever she pleased.

Having pinpointed the behavior which the counselor and teacher agree needs modification, proceed to the hypothesis generated by observation of that student's behavior. In the case of Jane, the target behavior was pinpointed as "blurting-out". It was hypothesized that if Jane contracted to keep track of her "blurting-out" behavior in a self-report and if she were offered a reward and reinforcement from her teacher and her counselor to modify her behavior in the English classroom, then she would change by not blurting-out and by doing her daily assignments.

It can also be hypothesized that the behavioral change will be satisfying to the student and that a change will occur in other classes, since pleasurable activities are usually repeated. In this case, the objective was first to increase the student's cooperative behavior, to let the teacher or students talk in class without Jane's interrupting, and to have her talk only after being recognized by the teacher. These were the objectives with which the counselor agreed to assist Jane.

MEASURING CHANGE

A frequency graph is one way to report data and analyze it. To pinpoint, we tell what behavior is being demonstrated, noting what the learner will be doing when he is demonstrating what he knows. Ambiguous words like "understand" or "appreciate" can be limited to acts that evidence those concepts.

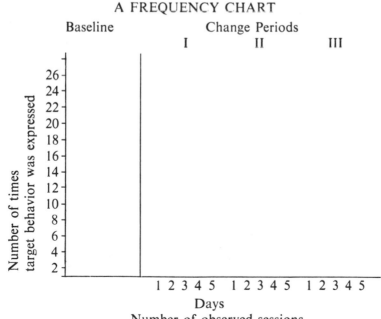

A FREQUENCY CHART

Days

Number of observed sessions

This chart might indicate the number of times the student disrupted the class by talking out. The first section of the graph is the baseline. This represents data obtained by unobtrusive observation. The target behavior is observed and counted. The time period of this recording should be long enough to determine a pattern of behavior.

Then, you might set the performance objective, enter into a contract with the student, and begin to record changes. Students can become trained observers. The student who is working on a change pattern can keep track of his own success. This strategy helps to reinforce his original commitment.

SAMPLE: Lateness Record

Day	1	2	3	4	5	6	7	8	9	10
Yes										
No										

STUDENT CONTRACTING

One strategy the counselor and teacher may use successfully to eliminate problem behavior is a contract with the student. Student contracting is a means of getting students to "operate" their lives.

According to Homme,[6] contracting should include these factors:

1. The contracts should call for a reward and accomplishments, rather than obedience.
2. Initial contracts should call for and reward small approximations of the desired behavior to assure success.
3. The performance should be rewarded after it occurs.
4. Rewards should be given frequently in small amounts.
5. Rewards on the contract payoff should be immediate.
6. The contract must be fair.
7. The terms of the contract must be clear.
8. The contract must be honest.
9. The contract must be positive.
10. The contract as a method must be used systematically.

---

[6]Lloyd Homme, *et al. How to Use Contingency Contracting in the Classroom* (Champaign, Ill.: Research Press, 1970).

JANE'S CONTRACT

I will participate in class when called on, but will not make any comments to students and/or the teacher even though they may annoy me or make me feel like interrupting them in the English class by "blurting-out." I understand that blurting-out means making angry or loud or interrupting comments when others are speaking and when I have not been recognized by the teacher.

It was also decided that a system of record keeping would be established for Jane: (1) She would keep a chart of her behavior each day in English class and record the times she "blurted-out" for three weeks thereafter. (2) She would keep an appointment with her counselor every Wednesday during this period to discuss her progress and to share information about her behavior.

The agreed upon rewards of Jane's contract, besides gaining her teacher's and counselor's approval, are described on page 230.

JANE'S SELF-REPORT ON BLURTING-OUT

	Monday	Tuesday	Wednesday	Thursday	Friday
February 8th to February 12th	卌 卌 ||||	卌 |||	||||	卌	卌 ||||
February 15th to February 19th	卌 |	|||	|||		||
February 22nd to February 25th	||		|||	|	Good Friday No school
March 8th to March 12th	||			|	

Jane reduced her "blurting-out" behavior to near zero frequency. She participated in class discussion and made comments only when she was recognized by her teacher.

To corroborate a student's self-report information, the counselor can observe for a few days each week and meet with the teacher during the last days of the contract. In Jane's case, the teacher was satisfied with the change she had made and felt that the self-report was fairly accurate.

REWARDS AND REINFORCEMENT

Some educators would argue that students should not be bribed to do what is expected. Indeed, why should we promise special favors to the disruptive, tuned-out youngster while most of the students perform their learning tasks in an acceptable way without reward?

Payoffs for wanted behavior are many in life. If we go to work each day, then we receive a paycheck. If we get along with others, we make friends that make us happy. However, self-motivation is what we ultimately seek to teach students. The problem is that self-motivation does not alway occur. This plan is an illustration of how the approach to modify Jane's behavior through rewards and reinforcement offered a possible solution, if not a definitive answer, to her particular case.

Jane was told by the counselor: "If you stop blurting out in English class, participate when called upon, and use self-control by not getting into heated arguments for the remainder of the grading period which is four weeks, I will help you secure a summer job with the Neighborhood Youth Corps program. Also, I will send a letter to your mother saying what an improvment you have been making in your English class." Jane and the teacher agreed to the terms.

The counselor consulted with Jane weekly to see how she was getting along on the contract. She encouraged her by offering Jane positive regard. Also, the counselor helped her with class assignments and to fill out an application for a Social Security card she needed for the job.

To encourage her to make better headway on the change program, the counselor suggested that if her self-report showed improvement, Jane would have the chance to get out of class for 20 minutes each week to discuss anything she wanted to. However, she was to be responsible for the work assigned in the class she missed. Also, she would have to keep faith with the objectives of the contract.

CHOOSING REWARDS

Rewarding good behavior is a payoff which results in students wanting to maintain that behavior. However, finding rewards that motivate is often a struggle. An interesting aside in Jane's case concerns the reward the counselor offered Jane for her change of behavior. Jane and her sister qualified for summer jobs in the federal program; however, so did about 2,000 other children, and only a few jobs were open. Jane confided in her counselor that she wished the counselor would help her get a job.

Jane's request was reasonable, but the counselor could not fulfill it. Fortunately, Jane understood that the counselor had done her best and accepted that effort as reward. Seeking desirable rewards is an ongoing process and requires much searching. *Be sure you only promise rewards that are reasonable and can be fulfilled.*

Occasionally a verbal reward of congratulations or accolades will suffice. Rewards can be words like, "That's good, you did a fine job;" expressions, like smiling or looking at students with acceptance and approval; or gestures such as a pat on the shoulder. With the defeatist, the potential dropout, the student might agree to attend class every day and learn to do certain designated tasks if he can be dismissed early on Friday for recreation.

How far we are willing to go on a contract to bring about change will depend on many factors. One important aspect is the degree of co-operation the teacher has from the school administration; another is the kinds of rewards that will be attractive, feasible and workable.

The use of rewards in contracting can begin small but become greater as successes are achieved.

Rewards are troublesome to those who feel that a student should perform because it is the "right" behavior, or that rewarding behavior is training for future disappointments, when social and work situations arise and there is no special payoff. However, as educators, we must constantly seek new strategies suitable to specific situations.

THE CARRY-OVER EFFECT

There was an observable change in Jane's behavior in science class noted by that teacher. Thus, there was a beginning of the carry-over effects of behavior modification. According to the counselor in our case study:

> Jane asked her mother to come to school to discuss some problems she had had with her science teacher and to find out why she had failed science for the last marking period. This was a new kind of response from Jane who usually didn't do much about a bad situation except gripe. Her mother went

to school and was very interested in Jane's improvement. Fortunately, the science teacher rewarded Jane for trying to find out how to improve by giving her extra help on a class project and by complimenting her on her efforts.

The counselor re-stated the contract with Jane and her self-report. She included Jane's keeping track of the number of times she felt like "blurting-out" in science, but didn't. The contract gave some indication of Jane's ability to control her actions and further reinforced her behavioral change.

Teachers can encourage students to record how they feel about themselves, how they think others view them and to discuss some of the hurt feelings and positive feelings they have. A diary can be a valuable instrument for both the student and the teacher. It can serve not only as a record of the student's school experiences, but can also unveil thoughts and feelings, give an indication of home life and relations with members of the family, and reveal dreams and aspirations.

> From Jane's diary, it was apparent that she had many apprehensions. Jane was living with a woman who she thought might not be her real mother, but possibly her grandmother. In one entry she indicated that she believed she had been adopted. (There was no evidence of such an arrangement.) There were ten children in the home and Jane was one of the four youngest.
>
> Jane did not feel comfortable around many of her peers. She was aware that some of them talked among themselves about her, and suspected that one had suggested to the counselor that she talk to her about using soap and a deodorant.
>
> Jane felt that she was being "picked on." She had been suspended from school four times during the school year because "she always wanted to fight." Her mother had refused to come to school to discuss problems and each time Jane was readmitted with promises to change.

The teacher can talk over feeling like these with students, and encourage them to build a supportive relationship with the teacher, the school counselor, or other responsive adult.

The teacher who is capable of taking on this role can help students learn that they are valuable and important human beings, that they are accepted for what they are and for what they may become. With this foundation of dignity and trust, they can learn to cope with most situations that are likely to occur.

Index